JUN - - 2013

Houdini Shots

Houdini Shots

The Ultimate Short-Game Survival Guide

MARTIN HALL
with
DAVE ALLEN

WILEY

All Seve Ballesteros photos © Leonard Kamsler; all Martin Hall photos by Fred Vuich © Martin Hall

Cover Design: John Wiley & Sons, Inc.
Cover Photographs: Front cover: © Mike Hewitt/Getty Images; Back cover: © Leonard Kamsler

Text design and composition by Forty-five Degree Design LLC

Published by John Wiley & Sons, Inc., Hoboken, New Jersey
Published simultaneously in Canada

Library of Congress Cataloging-in-Publication Data:

Hall, Martin.
    Houdini shots : the ultimate short-game survival guide / Martin Hall with Dave Allen.
        p. cm.
    Includes bibliographical references and index.
    ISBN 978-1-118-30837-0 (cloth); ISBN 978-1-118-48597-2 (ebk);
ISBN 978-1-118-48657-3 (ebk); ISBN 978-1-118-48658-0 (ebk)
  1. Short game (Golf) 2. Ballesteros, Severiano. 3. Golfers—Spain—Biography.
I. Allen, Dave. II. Title.
    GV979.S54H35 2012
    796.352'3—dc23

                                                                    2012025741

To the magician himself, Seve.
　　Those who saw you will never forget.

To my wife, Lisa: You are my everything.

To my Mum, Dad, and sister Gill: You always
　　encouraged me every step of the way. Thank you.

CONTENTS

FOREWORD by Jack Nicklaus

Due to changes in golf equipment over the years—a ball that goes longer and straighter, and equipment that puts greater emphasis on technology over technique—I am often asked whether there are still any true shotmakers in the game. The answer is yes. However, it is a different generation and vintage of shotmakers. Technology has taken the guesswork out of shotmaking: today's players can move the ball from left-to-right and right-to-left, and most important, can hit it straight thanks to the design of clubs and balls. In my day, it was almost impossible to hit a straight shot. We had to rely on maneuvering the ball—hitting it high or low, cutting it, hooking it. There was, at times, an artistry to shotmaking. Sometimes mystery. Sometimes mastery. And occasionally, even magic took center stage.

As history looks back and celebrates some of the best shotmakers our game has ever seen, there are few who rivaled or will rival the legacy of Seve Ballesteros.

I first came into contact with Seve in 1976 at Royal Birkdale. Johnny Miller won the Open Championship that year, and Seve and I tied for second. At the time, I knew very little about Seve. But from that point forward, I began to learn and admire so much about him. Seve became a force in the game of golf, with a record that legitimizes any accolade showered upon his legacy. His influence on the game, especially throughout Europe, where his passionate support of the Ryder Cup was second to none, was unparalleled. His artistry with club in hand was equally unmatched.

Seve brought great flare to the game. No matter the golf that particular day, you always knew you were going to be entertained. He was a champion for the common man and throughout the European continent for a game that was more of an elitist sport in his own country. It was his creativity, his imagination, and his desire to compete that made him so popular—not only in Europe but throughout the American galleries, too. You might say that Seve was a seat-of-the-pants golfer. He was able to invent shots that few others could, and he would play shots from anywhere—and did. When he won at Royal Lytham in 1979, he played the 16th hole from a car park (ironically, almost the same area Ernie Els played from during the final round en route to his 2012 Open victory). I have watched Seve hit 1-irons out of greenside bunkers when just fooling around. He could get up-and-down out of a garbage can, if the shot called for it. He could do *anything* with a golf club and a golf ball. Seve learned how to take the shots and the mentality he learned as a young boy in a caddie yard to a sophisticated golf course. He never changed himself; he learned how to adapt his game to the golf course.

I always shake my head when I hear players say that a golf course does not fit their game. In reality, it is up to the golfer to make his or her game fit the golf course. That was Seve.

For all of the success that I have been fortunate to enjoy, I would never consider myself a great short-game player. Certainly not the likes of a Seve. But I think any golfer—whether a high-handicapper or one at the highest level—has much to gain by mastering the short game. Seve provides us a great example, and through the eyes and words of Martin Hall in this book, we can all share in some of the secrets to Seve's success.

Martin has been a great friend for many years. When Jim Flick and I launched golf schools, we entrusted the role of lead instructor to Martin for many years. I also entrusted him to help some of my children and grandchildren, as well as countless friends. He is one of the top-ranked teachers by our friends at *Golf Digest,* and a former PGA of America Teacher of the Year. He has all the credentials any instructor could and should have. He has the eyes, the head, and, most important, the heart to help any level of player to improve. Martin has a passion for the game, which comes through in his interpretation of how Seve played. By revealing the method behind Seve's magic, Martin shows how the average golfer can benefit from these insights.

As Martin shares his thoughts in *Houdini Shots*, I hope you can share in some way, great or small, what made Seve Ballesteros so special in our game and to our game.

Good golfing,
Jack Nicklaus

ACKNOWLEDGMENTS

Seve Ballesteros was the most exciting golfer I ever watched play this game and was the inspiration for this book. I'm glad I witnessed him in full stride. To Dave Allen, my writer, we always said we would, and now we have! Thanks for your friendship over the years. A special thank-you to Stephen Power and my publisher, John Wiley & Sons, for making this book possible, and to my photographer, Fred Vuich, who made it so easy. Many thanks to Leonard Kamsler, as well, for all of the classic instruction photos of Seve, without which there would be no *Houdini Shots*.

To my great friend and confidant from Louisiana, Chuck Winstead, thanks for all of your support and the laughs. To the members from Trentham, especially Geoff, Keith, Blakey, Boughey, and Beech, many great memories of home. And to Ibis Golf and Country Club, thank you for allowing me to be me and to teach as I do. Special thanks to the Medalist Village Club and Spa, and especially to Cory Simon, for allowing us to photograph many of the short-game shots in this book.

To my students at Ibis, I hope that you've learned as much from me as I have from you. I've also had the good fortune to learn from the very best players and teachers in the game, and I thank them all for sharing their knowledge. A special thank-you to Bob Toski, Jim Flick, and Peter Kostis, who gave me my start in America. Finally, a huge thank-you to Jack Nicklaus, for all of the wisdom you have imparted on me. I feel very lucky to have learned from the greatest player of all time.

Introduction

The first time I saw Severiano Ballesteros was at the World Match Play Championship in 1975. At the time, I was an assistant professional at the Wentworth Club outside of London, and there was this young, dashing Spaniard with jet-black hair hitting balls on the driving range. I watched him for a few minutes and walked away, thinking, "Hmm, that's impressive," and then went about my business.

It wasn't until the following year that I really took notice of the same player who would soon become the Arnold Palmer of European golf. I was loosening up on the range in my very first European Tour event in Portugal, when suddenly I heard this extremely loud *thwack . . . thwack . . . thwack* sound emanating from behind me. It was a much different sound than I'd ever heard before, one I later learned could be created only if you are hitting the ball smack-bang in the middle of the clubface with a tremendous amount of clubhead speed. I turned around to see what it was, and there was Seve in a bright red Slazenger sweater, hitting shots the likes of which I'd never seen before. I can remember it to this very day.

I stopped hitting balls myself and watched intently for several minutes, something I would become accustomed to doing with Seve during the next thirty-odd years. I remember calling my dad from the course after missing the third-round cut, saying, "There's some Spanish chap named 'Boldarino' or 'Ballarama' or something other out here, and I'm going to follow him for a bit. He looks good to me." So I watched him over the final six holes and, when it was over, couldn't help but think, "Wow, if this is the future of European golf, then perhaps I better go back into teaching." Holes that I would hit a driver and a 6-iron to, he was cutting the corners on and driving his ball on the front of the green. There was one hole, about 520 yards, which was a driver-3-wood-pitching wedge for almost everyone in the field. Word got around the clubhouse that Seve knocked it on the green in two, which was unheard of back then with persimmon woods and balata balls. He was just so powerful.

Outside of Pedrena, Spain, and the players on the European Tour, few people knew just how good this nineteen-year-old was, or how good he was about to become. That all changed a few months later when he tied for second in the British Open at Royal Birkdale, finishing six shots behind Johnny Miller. From that moment forward, the whole world took notice, and his career took off like a rocket.

I never had the pleasure of playing with Seve, who passed away from brain cancer in May 2011, but I watched him hit hundreds and hundreds of balls, and not just on the range. I recall Seve and seven or eight of his fellow countrymen hanging around the practice green early one evening at the German Open, hitting all types of impossible chip shots for several hours. I don't know what they were playing for—a beer, a soda, bragging rights—but they were laughing and enjoying every moment of it like a group of young children on a playground. During one rain delay in Holland, they took their game inside the clubhouse, pushed aside some chairs, and took turns trying to pitch a ball into a round ashtray. Sometimes they would do it. It wasn't the easiest thing in the world to nip the ball off a bare carpet, but to Seve it seemed routine.

Although Seve could hit the ball farther than most people, it was his flair for the short game and his ability to create something out of nothing that made him stand out. Inside 60 yards, he was Houdini with a golf club. Anyone who watched or played against the Spaniard was left mesmerized by his finesse and shotmaking abilities around the green, which produced some of the bravest and unlikeliest recovery shots in golf history.

The great Jack Nicklaus mused how he once saw Seve hitting soft, greenside bunker shots with a 1-iron "just fooling around" in practice. Television commentator David Feherty recalled how Seve once thumped a 4-iron into the face of a cavernous bunker at St. Andrews, getting the ball to drop softly over the lip and trickle down just 4 feet from the hole. I'll never forget the pitch-and-run shot (what I like to call "the chip and bumble") he hit from just left of the green on the final hole at the '76 British Open, threading a 9-iron between two greenside bunkers and taking just enough speed off the ball to leave himself with a short 4-footer for birdie. The ensuing putt allowed Seve to tie Nicklaus for second.

Everyone from my generation has a favorite Ballesteros story, and it usually involves Seve pulling off some kind of short-game shot that nobody else in the world could fathom. Probably my favorite Seve story comes from Billy Foster, Seve's one-time caddie. Ballesteros had knocked his approach shot through the back of the 16th green at Wentworth, leaving himself with virtually no green to work with and seemingly no shot—because the flagstick was also positioned in the back. Billy turned to Seve and asked, "What do you think?" Seve replied, "No problem, I will hit the flag." A puzzled Billy thought he meant the flagstick, which was a risky play because the ball could deflect anywhere if it indeed hit the stick. What he didn't know was that Seve meant the actual cloth of the flag. Sure enough, Seve popped the ball up in the air, hit the flag, and landed the ball a few inches from the hole.

Who's to say where he learned that one? Perhaps it was during one of many late afternoons on the chipping green with the other Spaniards, or it was on the local golf course in his hometown of Pedrena, where he and the other caddies would rise before dawn and often attempt such unorthodox shots. One thing is certain: Seve wasn't afraid of any shot, and he had the imagination and skills to pull it off. Whether you were a fan, a budding young pro like myself, or a fellow competitor, you hung on every move he made.

"The imaginative player sees several ways to recover from a situation," Seve once said, "while the mechanical player sees only one."

Seve wasn't just a master of the impossible shot, he was a terrific putter, and his pitching, chipping, and overall play from inside 100 yards were brilliant. There was no one better in the late 1970s and throughout the 1980s at getting the ball up-and-down from around the green. And if that meant getting it up-and-down from the ball washer, he'd do it. Seve had an innate ability to put the middle of the clubface on the ball every time, no matter what the lie. He never mis-hit a short-game shot; thus, he had as good a short game as anyone who's ever played the game.

Said six-time major winner Nick Faldo, who like Ballesteros won three Open Championships: "For golf, he was the greatest show on earth. I was a fan and so fortunate I had a front row seat."

Ballesteros won eighty-seven times around the world, including five major championships, and played on eight European Ryder Cup teams. During one nine-year stretch from 1979 through 1987, Seve won forty-two tournaments worldwide, including four of his five major titles (the 1980 and 1983 Masters; the 1979 and 1984 British Open). He was far and away the best golfer in Europe during this period, and many would argue he was the most dominant player in the world.

During the 1980s, Seve served as a playing editor for *Golf Magazine*. His byline appeared on many instruction articles, most having to do with the short game. In 1986, *Golf Magazine* staff photographer Leonard Kamsler was sent to Spain to shoot a series of instruction tips with Seve under the tentative title, or theme, of "Houdini Shots." These would focus on some of Seve's greatest escape acts—from hitting the ball out from under the lip of a bunker to playing an intentional hook out of the trees. The story never ran, nor did any of the pictures, which you will see for the very first time in this book. The photos taken for this article were the inspiration behind *Houdini Shots*, which features more than sixty images of Seve in his prime, each in some small way providing a hint at his brilliance and, more important, just how he was always able to get himself out of trouble.

Seve was unquestionably the greatest shotmaker and innovator of his generation.

This is especially true when it came to the short game: Whether his ball was buried in a greenside bunker, nestled down in ankle-deep rough, or up against a tree, Seve found a way to get the ball on the green. As a result, he was one of the very best ever at playing "scoring golf." This is when you scuff your 3-wood down the fairway on a par 5, gouge the ball up to about 80 yards, stick your approach to 4 feet, and make your birdie. Most amateurs spend too much time working on their full swing, giving their short game and scoring skills no attention at all. Successful professionals do exactly the opposite—they spend a lot more time on the short game than they do on the full swing. Professionals are playing scoring golf, whereas amateurs are trying to play what I like to call "exhibition golf." When all is said and done, the score matters most.

I can't overemphasize the importance of a good short game. The great Phil Rodgers once said that "the two most important shots on a hole are always the last two." I couldn't agree more. Most people who shoot 85 or higher would be shocked if they really knew how poor their short game was. They're under the assumption that their driver or long game is responsible for their high scores, when it's really the three-putts, the duffed chips, or the poor bunker shots that do them in. The simple truth is, if you want to score well and improve in the fastest manner possible, you have to be good from 100 yards and in.

It's no surprise that two of today's greatest players—Tiger Woods and Phil Mickelson—also have two of the best short games in the world. That's how you win major championships, club championships, and state high school titles. Golfers who spend all of their time on the driving range trying to perfect their swing are missing the boat. What allows Tiger and Phil to shoot incredibly low scores is their ability to get up-and-down in two at several crucial times during a round. It keeps their momentum going. The short game lets you shoot 71 when you're not playing well, and 63 when you're playing really well. Relatively speaking, the same holds true for every golfer. The short game can definitely provide you with some valuable momentum, in that you can stop the bleeding with a good chip or putt and get back on track.

In *Houdini Shots*, you'll learn how to play more than fifty of the most difficult short-game shots in golf, many of them accompanied by photos of Seve, with my analysis on just how Mr. Houdini himself executed each shot. Because many of these shots involve quite a bit of risk—and an extreme degree of difficulty—I've also included tips geared specifically toward mid- and high-handicappers so that they can best extricate themselves out of trouble. Sometimes, getting the ball down in three—instead of two—is the best you can do. You save a bogey here and a double bogey there, and the "rescued" strokes start to add up. The key is to avoid those huge numbers that can cripple a score.

Besides teaching you how to score better, *Houdini Shots* will leave you with a greater arsenal of shots to choose from, which will give you the confidence to turn three or even four shots into two. If there's another thing I hope you take away from this book, it's that feeling that it's never over until it's over. Seve and all great short-game players shared this quality, which is to say that if you have a good imagination and attitude, you can pull a rabbit out of a hat at the last minute and make some magic of your own.

Martin's 7 Maxims of the Short Game

When I first started out teaching, I watched as much film of Seve's short game as I possibly could, and I spotted some definite patterns. For one, the time it took him to go through his pre-shot routine was the same whether he was chipping on the 72nd hole of the British Open or the 6th hole of the Wednesday Pro-Am. He'd walk in from behind the ball, holding the club with just his right hand, and shake the tension out of his left arm. Then he'd set the clubhead down about six inches away from the ball, put his left hand on the club, hitch up his pants, look at the target, look at it again, and go.

He was always so focused on the target. All of the great short-game players are—they stare at the target and glance at the ball. The average golfer, by contrast, stares at the ball and only casually glances at the target.

Perhaps Seve's greatest quality was his ability to make the most solid contact possible that the lie would permit. If you could imagine a dot on the back of the ball and another on the center of the clubface, he made them collide just about every time. He never mis-hit the ball. His hand-eye coordination was extraordinary.

The reason I bring up these traits of Seve's is because they constitute two of my seven maxims of the short game. Whether you want to become great at the short game or shave a few strokes off your scorecard, you need to follow these rules. Seve had a tremendous imagination, and he was supremely confident in his ability to execute shots most people would deem high-risk, but I believe he always adhered to these rules. As you practice the shots in this book and work to implement them into your own short game, refer back to these rules. If you do, your improvement will be much faster, and your scores will start to reflect it.

Maxim #1: Solid Contact Is Essential

The importance of making solid contact in the short game cannot be overstated. It's so important, I dedicated half a chapter's worth of drills to it (see chapter 7). To consistently hit the ball a predictable distance, you must make solid contact (see FIGURE 1.1). Now, in some instances you simply can't make flush contact with the ball (e.g., from the sand or the thick rough). When the ball is nestled down in several inches

1.1

of rough, you're going to catch a lot of grass between the ball and the clubface, and the distance—particularly the amount of roll—will be somewhat unpredictable. Still, whether you're hitting out of the thick junk or from the greenside bunker, you want to contact the ball in line with the center of the clubface. The more consistently you're able to do this, the more reliable your distances will be.

If you contact the ball all over the face, you won't be able to develop any sense of touch or distance, because you'll have nothing to refer back to—except a wide array of mis-hits and erratic distances. Yet if you know that your 9 o'clock backswing produces a 50-yard shot, because you consistently hit the ball solidly, then you can swing away with confidence any time you have to play to that yardage.

Distance control in the short game is more important than direction. If you chip the ball 3 feet left or right of the hole but the correct distance, you still have a good opportunity to get the ball up-and-down; however, if you chip it on line but well short of or past the hole, then you have your work cut out for you. When I watch most recreational golfers, I see more shots come up short than long, although some blaze past the hole. That's because most recreational golfers don't hit the ball solidly enough on a consistent basis.

Maxim #2: Use the Least-Lofted Club Possible That Will Land the Ball on the Green

There are some world-class players who use only one club to chip or pitch with—usually a lob or a sand wedge. If you played golf all day long and played on the PGA Tour, maybe you could, too. For most people, though, I recommend using the least-lofted club possible that will still land the ball on the green (see FIGURE 1.2). I prescribe to the theory of "minimum air time, maximum ground time." Why? Because it's much

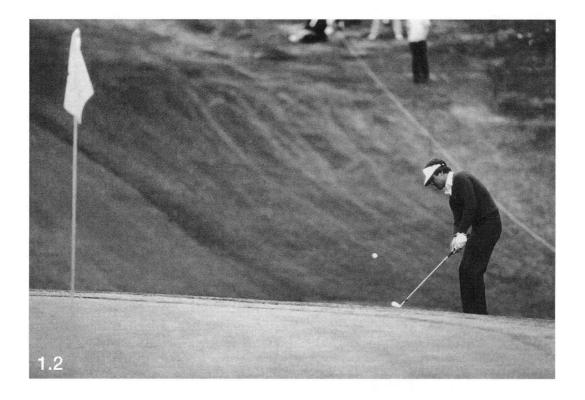

1.2

easier to judge the distance when rolling something along the ground than it is tossing it through the air. For one, you don't have to take as much swing, and second, the ball won't have as much backspin. If you're not sure which method is easier, try tossing ten balls underhanded at a flagstick 20 yards away—covering the entire distance in the air. Next, take ten balls and roll them along the ground at the same hole. See which set of ten balls finishes closer to the target. It's usually the roll.

A pitch shot with a sand wedge or a lofted club requires more wrist hinge and a bigger swing than a chip, and therefore has more room for error. A chip with a lesser-lofted club— say, a 7-iron—requires far less swing and is much easier to control because the clubhead has less distance to travel. In other words, it's easier to put the sweet spot of the face on the ball. Therefore, unless you have some obstacle to carry (e.g., a bunker or a heavy rough) or there's a fair amount of slope to navigate between you and the hole, you should always favor the chip.

The other advantage to keeping the ball low, besides needing less swing, is that you can keep your swing essentially the same. The feel of the swing doesn't change, only the choice of the club does. You control the amount of distance the ball flies in the air and rolls along the ground by the club's loft. A pitching wedge typically has a carry-to-roll ratio of 1:2; a 9-iron, 1:3; an 8-iron, 1:4, and so on. But when you choose to hit every shot in the short game with only one club, you have to vary the length of your swing, the ball position, and the attack angle to control the distance, which is too difficult for most people. By varying clubs, however, you keep the swing elements constant and you need less backswing. It's simple: the more swing you have to make, the more difficult you make it on yourself.

Maxim #3: Land the Ball on a Flat Surface

Whenever possible, land the ball on a flat area of the green, where the first bounce is likely to be straight and more predictable (see FIGURE 1.3). Landing the ball on a slope is a risky play, because the hill will often kill the ball's momentum and, in many instances, shoot it off-line. If the spot you want to land the ball on is hilly, then chip it over the slope or use your imagination and move where the front of the green (that is, your landing spot) is in your mind's eye. Also pay close attention to the grain of the green: if it's downgrain (the grass will appear shiny in color), the ball will often take off when it lands; conversely, if it's into the grain (the grass will appear darker), the ball will often hit the brakes when it lands. A good chipper takes all of these things—grain, slope, wind, firmness of the green, and so on—into consideration.

1.3

Most Tour pros land the ball one to two paces onto the green when chipping. This provides them a little margin for safety. You don't want to land the ball too close to the edge of the green, because if you come up short in the fringe, the bounce can be unpredictable. Most greens slope from back to front, too, so it's okay to carry the ball a little farther onto the putting surface, since you're chipping slightly uphill into the slope. If you land the ball on the edge of the green, you might come up short.

Maxim #4: Swing the Club along Your Shoulder Line

Should you need some height and stopping power, you'll want to open your stance so that a line along the toes and the shoulders points left of the target. Opening your stance helps impart more cutspin on the ball, so that it flies higher and drops more vertically from the sky, like a parachutist coming in for a landing. The ball may spin a wee bit to the right on landing, but it will stop much quicker than a standard pitch shot. This is useful when you're trying to lob the ball over a greenside bunker to a tight pin location, or you need some extra height to clear the lip of a bunker. Most shots in the short game are played from an open stance.

The higher and softer you want the ball to go, the farther you aim to the left and the more you swing to the left—on the plane of your shoulders (see FIGURE 1.4). The clubhead should always follow the line of your shoulders during the swing. This is important, because many golfers think that they should direct their swing at the target. Not so. Your shoulders are parallel to your swing's plane, or path, and the more you move your shoulders to the left, the more the plane moves to the

1.4

left. If you set up with your shoulders perfectly square to the target, then you will swing the club in the direction of the target. You should always swing on the plane of the shoulders; just remember that the plane isn't always aimed at the target.

Maxim #5: Have the Clubface Looking at the Target

When I speak of the target, I'm not necessarily referring to the flagstick. Your target could be a tree behind the green, a playing partner's marker several feet from the flagstick, the edge of a bunker, and so on. It's where you want the ball to start, and it's almost always where you want to aim your clubface (see FIGURES 1.5 and 1.6).

1.5   1.6

As an example, let's say you're hitting your third shot into the 10th green at Pebble Beach Golf Links. The green slopes sharply from left to right, toward the ocean, so any errant approach shot to the right is sure to find the beach below. About the only chance you have to wedge it close is to aim your clubface at the left side of the green, well left of the pin, and let the ball feed down toward the hole. If you aim the face directly at the flagstick—even with your feet and shoulders open to the target—the ball is going to land near the flag— probably to the right of the flag—and quickly run out of real estate.

The face angle at impact is largely responsible for the shot's initial starting direction (about 75–85 percent); therefore, if you aim your face at the flagstick, that's likely where it's going to start. Before you play your shot, make sure to examine the lie of the ball, the slope of the green, the position of the flag, the wind . . . anything that may affect the trajectory or the spin on the ball, how it rolls, and what your target will be. Don't always assume that the target is the flagstick—sometimes the best play is to aim 20 feet left or right of the pin. In this instance, adjust your target so that it's 20 feet away from the flag, and aim your clubface accordingly.

Maxim #6: See the Shot in Your Mind's Eye and Rehearse It

I detailed Seve's pre-shot routine earlier in this chapter. In a nutshell, he would spend most of his time (about 90 percent) looking at the target and visualizing the shot—its trajectory, how much the ball would spin and roll out, and in what direction (see FIGURE 1.7). All great players do this; in fact, Jack Nicklaus talked about how he'd see the shot like a movie in reverse, with the ball coming out of the hole and working its way back toward him. This visualization technique gave him something to react to, whereas the average recreational golfer stares at the ball and the ground and has no sense of where the target is or what he or she wants to do with the ball.

The secret to being really good at the short game is to elevate your awareness of the clubhead, the direction of the wind, the slope of the green (is it uphill or downhill?) and,

1.7

most important, the target. I recommend running through a really short pre-shot checklist, then taking several rehearsal swings off to the side of the ball. As you do this, visualize the shot as you want it to play out—see the trajectory, the precise landing spot, the run-out, and so on. Try to brush the ground with the club where the ball would be in your stance, or just ahead of it. Once you're done with your practice swings, set up to the ball, take one final look at the target, and go. Because of the connection you have to the target, you should have a good feel for the amount of swing you need to make to produce the desired result.

Maxim #7: The Lie of the Ball Dictates What's Possible

Seve was a very confident and aggressive player, but he wasn't foolish. If the lie was near impossible, and he didn't think he could put the club on the ball and hit a reasonably good shot, he wouldn't attempt it.

The lie is the very first thing you should examine when you arrive at your ball (see FIGURE 1.8). It, more than anything else, determines how you are to play the shot. If, on one hand, the ball has settled down in the rough, you're not going to be able to spin it very well, so you can forget about trying that super-high flop shot. You then need to look at other alternatives, such as pitching the ball 20 feet left or right of the pin or 25 feet beyond the hole. If, on the other hand, the ball is sitting reasonably well and you can get most of the clubface on it—or can slide the clubhead underneath it—then the high lob is something to consider.

When you encounter a very poor lie, always ask yourself, "What's my best chance to get the ball up-and-down in two?"

1.8

Sometimes, the best option might be to leave yourself with a 25- or 30-foot putt for par. The most important thing is to not bring double or triple bogey into the equation. Three shots can be okay; just don't make it four or five.

Think LOWER

Earlier, I mentioned the importance of having your own pre-shot checklist. This means gathering as much information as you can about the shot so that you can make a sound decision about which club to choose and what shot to play. When you step up to the ball, all of your thinking should be done. It's not the time to be indecisive; you should have a clear game plan for what you're going to do.

The following five-step pre-shot checklist is easy to remember because it's an acronym for the word LOWER. It's also very efficient—run through it several times on the practice range and the course, and it will become second nature to you.

L— First, examine the **Li**e of the ball. Is it sitting up in the grass or down? Is it above or below your feet? Is the ground firm or soft?

O—What **O**ptions are open to you? Preferably, you want to use the least-lofted club possible and keep the ball along the ground, but you might have to launch it up high to avoid a bunker or some other obstacle.

W—Is there any **W**ind, and, if so, in which direction is it blowing? Shots into the wind tend to roll a lot less, whereas shots downwind tend to take off.

E— How much **E**levation is there? If the shot is significantly uphill, you may have to carry the ball higher and farther and play more club; if it's downhill, you may want to hit the ball short of the green and let it trickle on, or hit the softest-landing ball possible. The slope of the green is also very important—if it slopes significantly from right to left, then you'll want to make sure to land the ball to the right of the flagstick and let it feed down to the hole.

R— When you're done examining all of the information, **R**ehearse your swing a few times to get a feel for the length of swing you need to make. Make sure to look at the target as you swing because your eyes are the best gauge of distance.

Short Game No-No's

Just as there are several must-haves in the short game, there are a few things you should absolutely try to avoid. Atop this list of no-no's is a strong grip (hands turned more to the right on the handle, with the V's formed by your thumbs and fore-fingers pointing toward your right shoulder). There are very few shots in the short game where you want the clubface turning over through impact, and that's exactly what the stronger grip encourages. With a strong grip, there's a tendency to drop the right shoulder too much on the downswing, instead of turning it through, which makes getting the bottom of your swing's arc to the ball or just beyond it very difficult. The shoulders tend to move up and down, instead of on a circular path similar to a tilted merry-go-round, and the result is a lot of fat and thin shots.

With a neutral grip (V's pointing toward chin), which Seve used, the face is more prone to stay square to open, and the shoulders will turn on a plane somewhere between vertical and horizontal. That leads me to another common short-game mistake, which is swinging the club off-plane. In order for the bottom of the swing's arc to hit the ground in the right place—directly under the ball or, sometimes, on the target side of the ball—the club has to be traveling on a circular arc. (Many of golf's best teachers refer to this as an inside to down-the-line to back inside path.) A lot of golfers think they should swing the club straight back and straight through, but that will only put the bottom of the arc in the wrong place, usually behind the ball. When you set up, make sure to position the ball at the bottom of your swing's arc (where you want the clubhead to touch the ground) or before it. Provided you swing the club on-plane, you should hit the ball solid.

Another thing you should never attempt to do is keep your body completely still. Golfers seem to blame every mis-hit on moving too much, whether it's lifting their heads prematurely or dipping down at the start of the downswing, so they compensate by trying to remain frozen on the next shot. Seve never tried to keep his head down—he'd hit the shot, and it would pop right back up. He had his feet, hips, knees, and shoulders moving all of the time, as do most good players.

The golf swing is an athletic movement, and the idea of trying to keep your head still or your spine angle constant is a bad thing. If you remain too static, then you have no momentum to move your arms back and forth. The job of the hands and the arms in the swing is to lift and lower the club, while the body's role is to move the club away from and toward the target. If you stand still, then you haven't got a body to move the club to and fro, and your arms have to do it. When you're forced to move the club toward the target with your arms, you're going to have a more difficult time making solid contact.

The last kiss-of-death philosophy I want to address is the idea that you should deliberately accelerate through the ball. Other than moving too much, the most common excuse golfers make for a bad shot is decelerating the club into impact. As a result, you get players standing still and overaccelerating their hands and arms into the finish. This is disastrous. You don't find acceleration with a hit from your hands and arms; you get it from the correct sequencing and pivoting of your body. As the body turns through, it pulls the hands and the arms along for the ride, providing the momentum they need to bring the club to a full finish. Acceleration: yes! Deliberate hand acceleration: certainly not!

How to Cash in Your Chips

Before I discuss how to play everything from the basic running chip to the floating chip, it's important that I distinguish the most notable difference between a chip and a pitch shot. Most people separate the two by the flight of the ball—that is, a chip rolls mostly along the ground, whereas a pitch travels a good distance in the air and rolls less. That's true, because chips do tend to roll out more, but another distinction is the amount of wrist hinge in both shots. In a chip, there's minimal to no wrist action, whereas in a pitch, the wrists do hinge. This cocking of the wrists creates an additional lever and more clubhead speed, which is what allows you to carry the ball farther in the air and have it roll less.

Whenever possible, it's easier and more reliable for most players to choose a chip over a pitch, using the least-lofted club that will land the ball on the green. There are two reasons for this: (1) a chip doesn't require as much swing or clubhead speed as a pitch, thus, there's less likelihood of a mis-hit; and (2) it's easier for most people to judge roll than to judge carry. Unfortunately, you're not always going to get a good lie to chip from, nor is the green going to be completely flat. Sometimes the pin will be positioned very close to you, and other times it will be a good distance away. My point is, although the chip is the most basic of short-game shots, a few situations will test your shotmaking skills and require a Houdini-like touch. Here are a few, with my observations on how Seve might've played each shot, and how you may want to tackle them as well.

Basic Running Chip

The standard chip is probably the easiest short-game shot to execute and among the most common. Yet, for every time I see one ball finish past the hole, I see at least ten finish short—sometimes well short. One of the main reasons for this is club selection—most golfers chip with only one club, usually a sand wedge, which forces them to make a bigger swing and mis-hit the ball more frequently. When you're only a few paces off the putting surface, and there's a fair amount of green between you and the flagstick, you want to play a less-lofted club, such as an 8- or a 9-iron, which will give you more roll. When struck correctly, most 9-irons have a carry-to-roll ratio of one part flight, three parts roll, which means if the ball carries 5 yards in the air, it will roll 15 yards along the ground.

A sand wedge has a carry-to-roll ratio of 1:1, a pitching wedge 1:2, an 8-iron 1:4, a 7-iron 1:5, and so on. Vary your chipping club, based on how much carry you need to land the ball onto the front of the green and how far you need it to roll out.

As far as technique is concerned, the thing that strikes me most about the photo of Seve here is how abbreviated his follow-through is. This suggests very strongly to me that there's no unnecessary acceleration or muscular effort at or after impact (see FIGURE 2.1). Why is this important? Because in terms of distance control, it's easier to judge distance through the length of the backswing, allowing a dead-weight, free-fall drop of the club and the arms so that gravity provides the correct amount of acceleration.

2.1

I also see that the shaft is still in line with his left arm after impact, and his right wrist remains bent back. He hasn't allowed the shaft to pass his left arm, which buys some insurance against any mis-hit at all. When you add loft to the face, the clubhead overtakes the hands too early, and you introduce the possibility of poor contact. You don't need to add loft on a chip—the club's manufactured loft is enough to get the ball up in the air—if you've chosen the right club.

Another thing Seve does well is that he turns his chest somewhat through the shot. His head rotates toward the target; it doesn't stay down. A lot of golfers stay completely still over this type of shot, which causes them to use their hands and arms too much. Your body pivot is largely what moves the club toward the target, and if you keep your body completely still, you can get very flippy-wristed with the shot.

What you don't see in this photo is Seve's right hand slipping off the club after impact, which I think is one of his trademark secrets. In order for this to occur, grip pressure cannot be too tight. Maybe the greatest common denominator among all superb short-game players is a fairly light and always constant grip pressure from start to finish. In fact, similar to Seve, many golfers (such as Fred Couples, Ernie Els) let their right hands slip off the club after impact. You don't want any sudden grabbing of the handle with the right hand, because that disrupts the club's acceleration and affects your distance control. Changing grip pressure within the motion also makes solid contact very unlikely.

MARTIN'S KEYS

- Play the ball back in your stance, opposite the inside of your right foot, and look at the top or front half of the ball, which will shift more weight to your forward leg. You can also lift your right heel off the ground some, which will ensure that your weight is on your left side.

- Don't consciously think about hinging your wrists on the backswing. Sometimes the weight of the clubhead will cause the wrists to give, but, for the most part, the basic running chip is a wristless stroke.

- As you swing through, make sure there's a little turn to your trunk; you don't want to keep your body completely still. Imagine that there's a big eye on your chest, and make the eye look somewhat at the target at the completion of your stroke (see FIGURE 2.2). I think it's a huge key to feel as if you're swinging the whole shaft and not only the clubhead.

- If the lie is poor (that is, sitting down in the first cut of rough), then you need to create a steeper angle of approach

2.2

into the ball to make solid contact. This lowers the effective loft of the club, so that your pitching wedge performs more like a 9-iron. The ball will come out on a slightly lower trajectory and roll more, so plan accordingly.

What if... You're 10 feet off the green, and there's 60 or 70 feet of green between you and the hole?

Some of the greens on the Old Course at St. Andrew's are the size of a football field, which can leave you with a pretty lengthy chip shot. You're not likely to play greens that big in America, but you may, on occasion, find yourself chipping with an enormous amount of putting surface between you and the hole. In these instances, don't be afraid to chip with a 5- or a 6-iron—the longer shaft produces more distance than a putter, so you don't have to take as big of a swing.

You can play "The St. Andrew's Runner" one of two ways: like a basic running chip or a hook chip. To execute the basic chip, play the ball just back of center in your stance, with your weight favoring

2.3

2.4

your front leg, and grip the club a little more firmly with the last three fingers of your left hand. The latter adjustment will encourage you to lead with the handle through impact, which ensures proper contact. Make sure you take a big enough backswing to get the ball to the hole, but don't follow through too much—your swing should feel like a wrecking ball running into a wall. It's okay to let your legs move some with the shot, just as they would with a long putt.

The advantage to the hook chip is that with the clubface closing through impact, it will impart less backspin on the ball than a square face would. As a result, the ball will have more overspin on it and run out more. To hit this shot, let the face open a little more going back (see FIGURE 2.3) and close a bit more going through (see FIGURE 2.4), like a swinging gate. As you're swinging through impact, try to get the toe to beat the heel to the ball. Feel as if your right palm is turning down through the shot, because this will help close the face slightly.

Chip Putt with a 9-Iron

Your ball comes to rest a few feet off the green, and you've got about 15 to 20 feet of real estate between you and the flagstick. This would be a good time to try the chip-putt technique, provided that the lie is fairly decent—that is, the ball is not buried or semiburied in the grass. Take your 9-iron, choke down to the metal so that your shaft is about the same length as your putter, and use your normal putting stroke. The reason you don't use a lob or a sand wedge in this instance is because you'd need to deloft the face considerably to land the ball just a few paces onto the green. This requires a steeper blow, which brings the chances of a mis-hit more into play.

2.5

One thing you'll notice about Seve is that there's some give to his elbows when he plays this shot (see FIGURE 2.5). His left wrist has also cupped just a little after impact, which means he's added loft to the face. The additional loft helps the ball come off softer, which is what you want when you face a short chip, as Seve does here. Seve looks to be using a 9-iron in the photo, which is why he can add loft and still land the ball where he wants, about two to three paces on the green. The cupping of the left wrist and the bending of the elbows also shallow out the path of the clubhead, so it's less likely to stick in the ground. This is worth a try, but is a technique usually best reserved for the experts.

MARTIN'S KEYS

- Position the ball in the center of your stance or slightly back of center, and grip down to the metal on the shaft for more control. Lift the heel of the clubhead just off the ground so that the shaft is on the same angle as that of your putter (see FIGURE 2.6)—that is, slightly more vertical. (The standard lie angle of a putter is about 71 to 72 degrees, whereas a 9-iron is 64 degrees.)

- Chip the same way that you putt, using your normal putting stroke. If you typically don't use your wrists when you putt, then don't use them when you chip, and vice versa. (If the pin is cut close or you're standing on a bit of an upslope, you may need to add some wrists.)

- Swing the club back and through on a slight arc, or inclined plane, not straight back and through. The shaft is on an angle and therefore needs to be swung on an angle. Make sure to turn your chest through so that it's somewhat looking at the target at the completion of your swing, and don't be afraid to use a little legs if the hole is a good distance away from you.

2.6

What if... The ball is sitting down in the rough, and you are less than two paces off the fringe?

If the ball has sunk to the bottom of the grass, the ground is relatively firm, and the hole is cut about ten paces onto the green, you might consider using your putter. With all of that grass behind the ball, it's extremely difficult to get the face of a sand or lob wedge on it, and judge the distance correctly. The putter allows you to make a smaller, more controlled swing and, with the proper setup adjustments, can be as effective as using a cue stick.

To play the putter chip, move the ball back in your stance so that it's several inches behind your right foot. The grip end of the club should point to a spot just outside your left hip. If the ball is behind your right foot, and the grip points outside your left hip, that will deloft the clubface at address to the point that it's looking at the ground (see FIGURE 2.7). It actually gives the clubface negative loft. Pick the clubhead up quickly and tap down on the back of the ball, banging it into the ground (see FIGURE 2.8). Provided that the ground is firm, the ball will pop out with a lot of topspin and then roll like a chip.

2.7

2.8

Chip from a Downhill Lie

When the lie puts you on a downhill slope, and the green is running away from you faster than a jackrabbit, you've got to use as much loft as possible. You may even want to address the ball off the toe, which will help soften the blow and deaden the run out. The most important thing from a technique standpoint is to swing with the slope. The front knee and shoulder have to stay down, because if the left shoulder comes up, you're going to lift the clubhead up, too, and hit the ball thin.

As you swing down the slope, have the feeling that your left knee stays flexed and your left shoulder turns low, as if it were moving under an imaginary bookshelf. Whatever you do, don't lift the bookshelf. As you can see in this photo of Seve taken at Augusta National, both of his knees remain down well past impact. His chest and head have released, and he's watching the flight of the ball (see FIGURE 2.9). He's not keeping his head down, which helps him turn his chest through and hit the ball solidly. If you keep your head down too long, then you run the risk of getting flippy with your wrists.

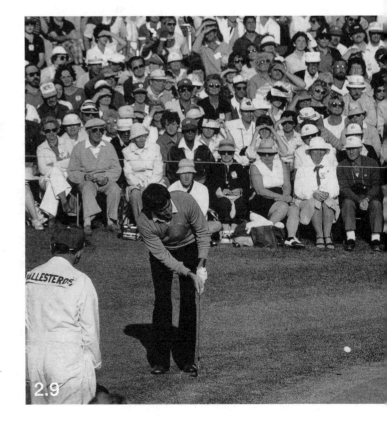

2.9

Ben Crenshaw, arguably one of the greatest putters of all time, said, "Once I've started the putter in motion, it's as if it's swinging itself." The same feeling should apply to a super-fast downhill chip—you don't want to add any unnecessary speed to the club on the way down, just let it swing itself.

MARTIN'S KEYS

- Place the ball in the middle of your stance and have the feeling that your weight is leaning down the slope (see FIGURE 2.10). It's similar to skiing downhill—the steeper the slope, the more you have to lean down the hill. You have to fight your instincts to pull up; otherwise, you'll fall on your bum.

- Choke down a few inches on the grip, and open both your stance and the clubface to add loft. Make sure the clubface is open to your body, or stance line, because this will help the ball ride up the face and come off a little softer.

- Swing the clubhead down the slope (see FIGURE 2.11), chopping the legs out from underneath the ball as if you were trying to hit the very bottom dimple on the ball. Don't contact the ball anywhere near the equator; instead, stay near the South Pole. Provided that the face is open and you swing along the slope, you can still slide the clubhead under the ball—even from a tight lie.

2.10

2.11

What if... The slope is really severe?

The more pronounced the slope is, the softer you have to hit the shot. You need to practically float the ball up in the air; otherwise, it will land and surely roll off the green. To hit a "floating" chip, aim your feet and shoulder lines well left of your target, open the club-face to your body (that is, the face should point somewhere to the right of your stance/shoulder line), and swing the clubhead down the slope, cutting across the ball as if you were hitting a cut-spin shot in ping pong or tennis (see FIGURE 2.12).

To help you slide the clubhead under the ball, feel as if the knuckles on your right hand are brushing the ground after impact (see FIGURE 2.13). The ball should run across the face, from the center out toward the toe, and come off as if you were tossing an egg underhanded to someone. The goal is to make a somewhat glancing blow by design, which will help soften the landing.

2.12

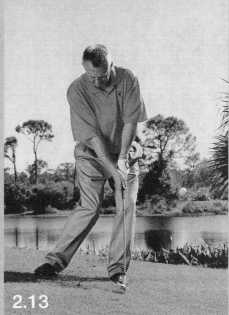

2.13

Chip from an Uphill Lie

At Augusta National, where the fairways and the greens look as if they may have some elephants buried under them, you'll rarely see the pros chipping from a flat lie. Uneven lies abound, and if their approach shot comes up short of the green, they'll frequently find themselves chipping uphill. In the photo here, Seve makes no attempt to keep his left arm straight and in line with the shaft after impact. You see some give to his left elbow, which suggests there's very little tension in his arms and shoulders (see FIGURE 2.14). By the abbreviated nature of his follow-through, I'm guessing Seve has pinched the ball off the slope here. This puts more spin on the ball and gets it to sit down faster, which is often necessary on the fast, treacherous Augusta greens.

There are two ways to play the uphill chip: (1) you can set up with your hips and shoulders parallel to the slope and swing up the slope, in which case you won't take much divot and the ball will come off higher; or (2) you can lean into the slope and play the aforementioned pinch shot, which will create a lower trajectory with more bite. For the average golfer, I'd recommend the former technique, because it allows you to make your more natural swing. If you try to trap the ball against the turf, you increase your chances of mis-hitting the shot.

2.14

MARTIN'S KEYS

- Play the ball in the middle of your stance and match your body to the slope, so that your spine is about at a right angle to the hill (see FIGURE 2.15).

- When swinging with the slope, take less loft than you ordinarily would from that distance. If you normally hit a 9-iron, then use a 7- or an 8-iron, depending on the severity of the slope. The uphill nature of the lie will increase the effective loft on the face at impact, making your 9-iron perform much as a pitching wedge or sand wedge does. If you don't switch, then you'll have to make a bigger swing to carry the ball the appropriate distance.

- Make no conscious effort to hinge the wrists, because the weight of the clubhead will do that for you. Let your knees, hips, and chest turn a little through the shot, and allow the clubhead to chase up the slope (see FIGURE 2.16).

2.15

2.16

What if... The pin is cut just over the edge of a steep embankment?

Your approach shot falls off the green and rolls down a steep embankment, leaving you with little chance to stop a pitch shot close to the hole. Seve found himself in this predicament on the 72nd hole of the 1976 British Open at Royal Birkdale. Needing a birdie to tie Jack Nicklaus for second place, he hit his second shot left of the green. The pin was cut in the front left corner of the green, not far from where Seve's ball came to rest. Rather than play some kind of lob shot, Seve took out his 9-iron and chipped the ball up the embankment, threading two greenside bunkers that guarded the pin. The ball hit into the slope short of the green, killing most of its forward momentum, and trickled down toward the flag, finishing just 4 feet short of the hole. Seve made his birdie and, in the process, gave the world a glimpse of his short-game wizardry.

First of all, for you to play any kind of "chip-and-bumble" shot such as this, the ground has to be firm enough to allow you to run the ball through it. If it feels soft or mushy and obviously is not firm, then you probably want to pitch the ball left or right of the flagstick—wherever there's more room. Play the ball back in your stance, just beyond your right foot, and hinge the wrists up quickly, tapping down on the ball as if you were trying to drive a tack into it (see FIGURE 2.17). The lower you want to hit

the ball, the farther you should position the ball back in your stance and the more you want to hit down on it. This is an extremely risky play, so don't try it unless you're desperate to make something happen, or you've practiced it as many times as Seve likely did.

5-Iron Trap Runner (from 20 yards)

If you find yourself with a fairly large greenside bunker blocking your path to the green, and you're not confident in your ability to pitch the ball safely over the bunker, you could run the ball through the trap. It's a very high-risk shot, and it will work only if the sand is firm and the lip of the bunker is fairly low, but it's worth a try if you've exhausted all other possibilities.

Seve is using a 5-iron in this picture, which can be good for creating plenty of topspin. As you can see, there's some hinge to Seve's wrists (see FIGURE 2.18), but not a lot of arm swing. He's fairly centered over the ball, with his weight favoring his front side. At the start of the downswing, he'll shift some more weight onto his left leg, which will help him trap the ball and lower its trajectory so that it comes out with a lot of roll. The ball will need to have some speed on it if it's going to run though the trap and onto the green, so solid contact is vital.

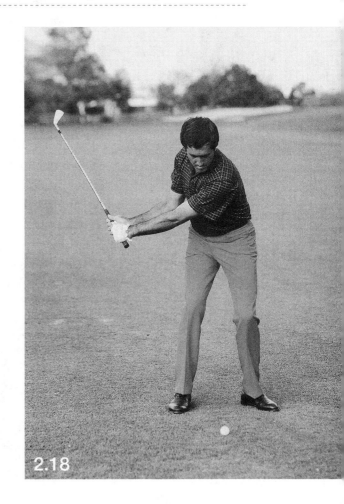

2.18

MARTIN'S KEYS

- To play this shot, the sand must not be powdery or fluffy, and the lip on the far side of the bunker must not be too steep. If it's several feet high or there's a steep face to contend with, then try an alternative shot.

- Play the ball back in your stance, opposite the inside of your right foot, and aim your feet, knees, hips, and shoulders to the right of your target. Close the clubface relative to your body lines, or aim.

- This shot is a miniature version of a hard hook. Keep the face looking at the ball during the takeaway, but on the forward swing, have the feeling that the toe of the club is speeding up and the face is turning down through impact. Imagine that you're wiping spilled milk off a table with your right hand—this will help you turn the face over and impart some topspin on the ball. It's just like skipping a rock across a pond: the more it hooks, the faster it scampers across the water—or, in this instance, the sand (see FIGURES 2.19 and 2.20).

2.19

2.20

What if... You are 15 yards off the green, and the pin is cut at the very back of the green?

The location of the flagstick has a big say over what type of shot you want to hit into the green, especially when you're within wedge distance. Ben Hogan used to say that if the flag was up front, he'd hit the ball in high; if it was in the middle of the green, he'd play a normal trajectory shot; and if it was back, he'd bring it in low. If it's well back, you don't want to take it in too high because you could easily overshoot the green and find yourself pitching uphill from behind the green, with no green to work with.

To hit a low bump-and-run shot to a back pin location, you need to land the ball on the front of the green and let it release and scoot back to the hole. Choose a lower-lofted scoring club, such as a pitching wedge or a 9-iron, and make a swing with very little wrist action. Imagine that someone has poured water over your hands and wrists, and the water has frozen; then swing back and through without cracking the ice (see FIGURE 2.21). With your wrists in ice, you won't be able to hinge your wrists, thus decreasing the likelihood of a mis-hit. Over the years, I've found this to be a very helpful image, because it improves the likelihood of your hitting the ball more solidly.

2.21

Pitching from 50 Yards and In

There were few better pitchers of the ball in his day than Seve Ballesteros, who crafted his short game by hitting every shot imaginable growing up as a youngster in Pedrena, Spain. When you can loft a 3-iron 30 feet up in the air and land it softly, then take the same club and run it along the ground and still get it close, you can pretty much name your short-game shot.

From 50 yards and in, Seve could make the ball do seemingly whatever he wanted it to—fly low and hard or high and soft—from any lie. He had a tremendous feel for these shots and knew how to manipulate both the clubface and his body to create the desired trajectory and ball flight he wanted.

Said former Masters champion Fuzzy Zoeller of Seve's unique ability to fit any shot to any situation: "Seve has the best touch from 50 yards and in I have ever seen."

I don't ever remember Seve losing a tournament from inside 50 yards, but he certainly won a few because of his ability to pitch the ball. Here's a little insight into how he played a variety of pitch shots, from the standard pitch to the short, extra-soft lob to the pop shot out of the rough. I'll even explain how he was able to put height on the ball from a severe downhill lie. In addition to these shots, I'll help you overcome your fear of tight lies and show you how to escape from high, wiry grass.

From 50 yards and in, you should be able to land the ball on the green most of the time, barring a horrible lie. With the right set-up adjustments and some knowledge of how Seve played these shots, you should also be able to get up-and-down more often, and save a multitude of strokes around the green.

Standard Pitch

With the possible exception of the greenside chip, this is the one short-game shot you'll encounter most frequently. If you can't play this shot, then you're going to struggle with your game inside 50 yards. Good contact is a must. Ideally, you want to contact the ball and the ground simultaneously, or the ball and then the turf. If the bottom of your swing's arc is too far behind the ball—or, in rare instances, too far ahead of the ball—you'll hit the shot fat or thin.

Seve was known as one of the greatest pitchers of all time, but his technique was a bit unorthodox compared to today's standard pitching practice. He would set up with his weight favoring his front side and would also flare his left foot out to encourage the correct leg and hip action through the shot. The importance of the lower body shifting and rotating is that it helps put the low point of the swing at the ball. Seve took a steep backswing but would then shallow out the clubhead's angle of approach by the time it reached the ball. He did this by rocking even more weight onto his front leg at the start of the backswing (see FIGURE 3.1) and moving his legs toward the target on the downswing. In his case, this created a slight reverse pivot, with his upper body and head both falling back slightly behind the ball before impact (see FIGURE 3.2). As a result, Seve was able to slide the club under the ball and hit it high and soft, with pinpoint control. It was as if he was tossing the ball underhanded at the target.

From my observations, Seve did not like hitting down on the ball and taking deep divots, unless he had to. At most, they were thin bacon strips. In general, the less divot you take, the more likely you are to return the club to the ball with the same loft you started with at address. If you're taking divots the size of a pork chop, then there's too much shaft lean present at impact, and your effective loft will be less. The ball will come out lower, which, for the average golfer, is bad because they don't generate a lot of spin. I think people who pitch the ball best just brush the ground, which is what Seve did by shallowing out his angle of attack.

3.1

3.2

MARTIN'S KEYS

- Play the ball in the center of your stance, measured from the inside of your heels. Focus on the top of the ball, which encourages your weight to shift to your front side (about 60–40 percent).

• As soon as you start to move your arms and shoulders on the backswing, have the feeling that you're pushing down with your left hand and pulling up with your right, only with some arm swing and body turn (see FIGURE 3.3). This cocking of the wrists helps create enough speed to hit the ball the desired distance without your taking a big swing. It also makes it easier to hit the ball and the ground at the same time. If there's little or no wrist hinge, it's difficult to get enough speed to produce the height you're looking for in a pitch shot. Also, you risk coming in too shallow, resulting in your hitting up on the ball and maybe catching it thin.

• On the way back, when your arms stop swinging, make sure your hips and shoulders stop turning, too. You want everything to stop moving at the same time, so that they

can all start down together—very different from the full swing. Synchronized is something I'd never suggest for the full swing but would always recommend for the pitch shot, because it allows for more control. In the full swing, you want to be sequenced, because that's how you generate more power.

- As you change direction, have the feeling that your arms are dropping as if under the influence of gravity; do not consciously add any acceleration to the arms (see FIGURES 3.4, 3.5, and 3.6). Your knees, hips, arms, and shoulders should all move back and through together. An image I use is that of rocking a bucket of water back and forth—you don't want your hands and arms moving independently of the rest of your body, or you'll spill the water. Your arms are responsible for moving the club up and down, while

3.5

3.6

your body's job is to move it back and forth. The better you're able to blend these two movements together, the more efficient your pitch swing will be and the easier time you'll have controlling your distances.

Drill: Hit the Runway

Place two tees on the ground, side by side, about a foot in front of a ball (see FIGURE 3.7). Set up to the ball as normal, and make a 9 to 3 o'clock pitch swing, bottoming the clubhead out just under the ball. The clubhead should brush the ground and then come back up again, missing the two tees entirely (see FIGURE 3.8). It's like an airplane about to land on a runway: the wheels touch down just momentarily and then lift up briefly. You don't want the clubhead to dig or stay in the ground for too long; otherwise, you'll hit the tees. The shaft will have too much forward lean to it, which means the club-face will have less loft on it than it started with at address. The purpose of this drill is to shallow out your angle of attack and stop you from digging. The best pitchers in the world don't take much of a divot and always bottom the clubhead out at the ball.

3.7

3.8

What if... The lie is tight, and you have to carry a hazard?

This is a scary proposition for many golfers and not just because of the bunker or the water that looms ahead, but because of the lack of a cushiony surface underneath the ball. Most weekend golfers would prefer to have some grass underneath the ball, because they feel more confident of their ability to slide the club under the ball and get it airborne. With a tight lie, however, there is no cushion, and the margin for error is much less than from the rough. As a result, there's a tendency to try to help the ball up into the air, which only brings the likelihood of a mis-hit more into play.

From a tight lie, you must have the low point of the swing either even with the ball or slightly on the target side of the ball. It's as if you're trying to knock the legs out from under the ball. Another analogy would be like that of shoveling snow out from under the ball, because the angle of attack needs to be fairly shallow (see FIGURE 3.9).

(CONTINUED)

3.9

53

(CONTINUED)

To hit down hard on the ball as if you were driving a stake into the ground is not only unnatural, but, at best, it leads to a low shot that makes the distance harder to control. You want to make a shallow, yet slightly descending, blow that hits the ball and the ground at the same time.

To hit this shot effectively, position the ball slightly forward of center in your stance, opening your feet and shoulders to your target. Lean the shaft back slightly, which will result in the grip end being closer to the ground than normal in your address position. The higher the shot required, the more your hands need to drop behind the ball and the farther you stand away from the ball. Make a few practice swings off to the side of the ball, on a line that's perpendicular to your target line, so that the actual ball is sitting on this imaginary line. Try to make every practice swing bottom out at the imaginary line, then move straight into the actual ball, take one last look at the target, and swing. Do not underestimate the power of this seemingly simple routine. It's helped thousands of golfers put the bottom of the swing in the right place, and make solid contact.

3.10   3.11

Drill: Coin Flip

Lay a silver dollar or another large-size coin on the ground, and practice hitting down on the coin so that it flips straight up in the air, not forward (FIGURES 3.10 and 3.11). The only way to get the coin to fly straight up in the air is to bang down hard on it with the sole of the clubhead. If you hit too far behind the coin, it will either jump forward or go nowhere at all. This drill teaches you how to get the bottom of your swing in the right place—at the ball—which is crucial when playing from a tight lie. On the course, feel as if the sole is touching down first, a fraction behind the ball, and you should be able to slide the clubhead under the ball and hit it high and soft.

Short, Extra-Soft Pitch

Now you've done it! You've hit your approach shot left of the green, on the same side that the pin is cut. There's only 30 yards between you and the flagstick, and the hole is cut about 10 paces onto the green. It's your classic "short-sided" situation, and to get the ball close, you'll have to hit the ball as delicately as possible, with as much loft as possible.

3.12

In the photograph, you can see that Seve's right hand has come completely off the club on his follow-through (see FIGURE 3.12). This tells me there's no energy left in the handle when he hits the ball, and his swing is free of tension. The clubface is also open to his body, which weakens the loft on the face so that the shot will come off higher and softer. His feet and shoulders are pointing well left of the ball's starting direction; therefore, his swing plane is also to the left, and the clubhead is cutting across the target line from out to in. This allows him to slide the clubhead underneath the ball, creating maximum height.

With a short, extra-soft pitch, you want to hit what I refer to as the "South Pole" of the ball, or the very bottom dimple on the ball, which will loft it gently upward. This weak, glancing blow is very different from a driver swing, in which you're trying to get the sweet spot of the club to hit the equator of the ball and launch it powerfully forward. The more you're able to slide the club under the ball, the higher the ball will go and the softer it will land.

MARTIN'S KEYS

- Start by aiming your body left of your chosen target, and point the clubface at your target. The ball should be slightly forward of center in your stance. Lean the handle back some so that your hands are slightly behind the ball.

3.13

3.14

- Make a normal backswing for a shot of about 30 yards (or whatever the distance might be), and as you swing down, feel as if you're throwing the clubhead under the ball and chopping its imaginary legs off. Any time you want maximum height, you have to let the clubhead pass your hands early. Your hands should be slightly behind the ball at impact, just as they were at address.

- To help you slide the clubhead under the ball, imagine that the head of a toothbrush is attached to the back of the club, just behind the toe area (see FIGURE 3.13). As you swing through impact, try to get the bristles on the toothbrush to brush the ground (see FIGURE 3.14). This will increase the loft on the club and get you to contact as few dimples as possible, resulting in a high-flying, soft-landing shot.

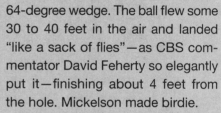

What if... You have zero green to work with, and only the highest of shots will stop the ball within 20 feet of the hole?

I might as well go ahead and name this the "[Phil] Mickelson Flop," for the left-hander with a penchant for hitting this high-flying daredevil of a shot. Few people in the world, besides Mickelson, can pull this shot off on a regular basis. Mickelson makes it look routine. During the third round of the 2012 Masters, Mickelson hit his approach shot on the par-5 15th through the green. The pin was cut precariously close to Rae's Creek, in the left corner of the green, but that didn't deter Lefty from taking a giant rip at the ball with his

3.15

64-degree wedge. The ball flew some 30 to 40 feet in the air and landed "like a sack of flies"—as CBS commentator David Feherty so elegantly put it—finishing about 4 feet from the hole. Mickelson made birdie.

As this play-by-play illustrates, you need to take a big swing to execute this shot correctly. The higher the shot, the more swing and clubhead speed you need, which will give you more spin. Set up with your hands behind the ball and the back of the club lying almost flat on the ground so that the clubface is pointing virtually straight at the sky (see FIGURE 3.15). The face should look like a pancake. Aim your body well left of the target so that the face is very open to your body, and swing away at full speed. This is the biggest, fastest swing you'll want to

(CONTINUED)

(CONTINUED)

make with a wedge around the greens. To generate speed, your swing needs to be full on both sides, so try to get your thumbs to your right shoulder on your backswing, and return them to your left shoulder on the forward swing.

Any time you want to hit the ball super-high, you also have to put additional loft on the club—more than the manufactured loft that's engraved on the sole. You need that 60-degree wedge to perform as if it has 70 degrees on it at impact. To help you create this additional loft, picture a cell phone in your right hand, and, as you swing back, rotate the clubface open so that you can see the numbers and dial 9–1–1, if necessary (see FIGURE 3.16). Then, as you swing through, keep the clubface pointing to the sky so that you can once again read the numbers (see FIGURE 3.17). You don't want the face squaring or turning over through the shot, because that takes valuable loft away.

3.16

3.17

3.18

After you contact the ball, immediately let go of the club with the last three fingers of your left hand—something Seve frequently did (see FIGURE 3.18). This encourages the clubhead to pass the handle prematurely and slide under the ball, popping it straight up into the air (see FIGURE 3.19). The super-high flop is not a shot for the faint of heart, so unless you have no other option but to throw the ball way up in the air with spin, leave it to the pros.

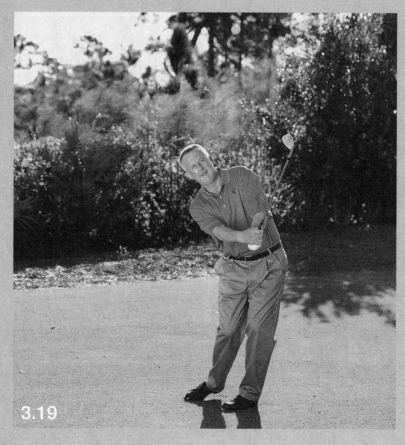

3.19

Pitch from a Severe Upslope

What's most interesting about this shot is how Seve's hips are almost horizontal and not parallel to the slope (see FIGURE 3.20). Traditional instruction for an uphill pitch says to always stand with your knees, hips, and shoulders parallel to the slope. Seve's shoulders are running with the slope, but because of the severe nature of the upslope, he's had to significantly shorten his left leg so as not to lose his balance. Almost all of his weight is on his front foot, but his spine is about perpen-

3.20

3.21

dicular to the slope, give or take a few degrees. He also looks as if he's digging his feet in as much as possible to help with balance and stability.

Because of his setup, Seve is going to swing more into the slope, rather than up the slope, which is the standard protocol when the lie isn't as severe. He'll chop down on the back of the ball with little to no follow-through, focusing on solid contact (see FIGURES 3.21 and 3.22). Because he's hitting down into the slope, the ball will come off on a slightly lower trajectory, so he'll play his most lofted club here, probably a sand wedge (see FIGURE 3.23).

MARTIN'S KEYS

- Assuming the slope isn't too severe, play the ball slightly forward of center in your stance, toward the higher foot, with your hips and shoulders parallel to the slope, your head behind the ball, and your weight favoring your back foot. Do not lean into the slope.

- Balance is key: Make a short, controlled backswing (see FIGURE 3.24) and swing the clubhead smoothly up the slope,

3.24

keeping your weight back behind the ball. In extreme cases, you would hit into the slope and tap down on the ball, but in this instance, you should feel as if the clubhead is sweeping along the ground. To help with balance, imagine that there's a tray of teacups on top of your head as you swing, and that you want to keep them from falling and spilling. If you rush your swing or jerk the club around, you risk hitting the shot fat.

- When swinging up the slope, consider dropping down to a 9-iron or even less loft so as not to shoot the ball up your left nostril. The angle of the slope plus the angle of the clubface equals your effective loft, so your 60-degree may play more like 80 or 90 degrees if you're not careful.

Pitch from a Severe Downhill Slope

Most amateurs have a more difficult time with this lie than they do pitching from an uphill slope. Because the slope is taking them downhill, they tend to lean back in an attempt to help the ball up into the air, causing the clubhead to bottom out too soon. They fight the inclination to move with the slope because it's easier to maintain their balance by falling in the other direction.

Seve, as he did with the uphill lie, does not set up with both his hips and shoulders parallel to the slope. Again, this has to do with the severity of the slope. He's kinked his right knee in and, in the process, managed to have his legs in a downhill position—nearly matching the slope—and his upper body almost in an uphill position. He's also pulled his right foot back some. These setup adjustments allow him to slide the clubhead underneath the ball without his body getting too far ahead of the ball (see FIGURE 3.25). In other words, he's figured out a way to get some height and stopping power on the ball from a lie that makes the two extremely difficult to accomplish.

3.25

What if... The ball is severely below your feet, and you need to carry it 20 yards to reach the green?

You can find this shot on courses with grass bunkers or grass faces for bunkers. The difficulty lies with maintaining your balance throughout the shot, because you'll be swinging from an extremely bent-over position. In this picture of Seve, he's so bent over that his spine is practically parallel to the ground (see FIGURE 3.26). As a result, the plane of his shoulders is going to be very steep and his swing almost straight up and down, like a Ferris wheel.

To pull off this shot, distribute more weight on your heels at address to counterbalance your upper body's weight going forward, and flex your knees to help the clubhead get down to the ball. Pick the club straight up on the backswing and drop it straight down into the back of the ball, as if you were chopping wood. This is the only way you're going to get any acceleration on the clubhead. As you swing, try to keep your chest pointing straight down at the ground. It's going to be nearly impossible to bend over any more without falling on your face, but as long as you don't raise up out of your spine angle, you should make decent contact.

3.26

MARTIN'S KEYS

- Assuming the slope isn't too severe, play the ball slightly back of center in your stance, toward the higher foot, with your body parallel to the slope and your weight favoring your front foot. Pull your right foot back some, away from the target line, to help with balance.

3.27

- Lean with the slope, and swing down the slope with the clubhead finishing low and down the hill. Slide the clubface under the ball, but do not consciously try to elevate the ball. Picture one dimple on the bottom of the ball, and try to make as little contact with the ball as possible, as if you were peeling the thin skin off an orange (see FIGURE 3.27). Finish with the fingernails on your bottom hand (right for right-handers) pointing toward the sky to maintain a weak loft on the clubface (see FIGURE 3.28).

- You can still slide the club under the ball from this lie, but because your body is so far forward at impact, you won't

3.28

get a super amount of loft on the shot. Use your most-lofted wedge and plan for the ball to come out low without too much spin on it.

Pop Shot from Long Rough

If you've missed your mark by 10 yards, and you encounter a rather gnarly lie with the grass growing against you, you've got one of two options available to you, depending on the amount of green there is between you and the flag. If you have a lot of green to work with, there's the cock-and-pop method, which Seve looks to be demonstrating here (see FIGURE 3.29). If there's very little green to navigate, then you have to open the clubface and play it like a bunker shot.

MARTIN'S KEYS FOR COCK AND POP

- This is the safest of the two options, because it doesn't require as big a swing, but you do need a fair amount of green at your disposal. Set up with your weight left, clubface square, and the ball opposite the inside of your right heel. Look at the front edge of the ball to ensure that your upper body leans forward slightly and your weight favors your front side (about 60–40 percent).

3.29

- Pick up the club quickly, cocking your wrists so that the shaft swings past parallel (or 9 o'clock) on the backswing. Pop down on the ball with very little follow-through, keeping your hands ahead of the clubhead through impact.

- Let your knees and legs move somewhat toward the target on the downswing, as Seve demonstrates in the previous photo. This should put the bottom of the swing arc in the right place and should eliminate the possibility of catching too much grass between the clubface and the ball. The ball will come out with very little backspin, so expect it to release and roll a good distance.

MARTIN'S KEYS FOR BUNKER SWING FROM THE GRASS

- If you're playing to a short pin from the thick stuff, then you're going to have to manufacture some loft so that the ball lands as gently as possible. Play it like a greenside bunker blast—set up with the ball forward, your hands back, and the clubface open to your body lines. Your stance should point you left of the target (which doesn't necessarily have to be the flagstick), with the face aimed at your target.

- Take about a three-quarter-length backswing and swing the clubhead down along your shoulder line, cutting across the target line from out to in. Imagine that the ball is sitting on a tee, and knock the legs out from under the ball, just as you would on a bunker shot.

- You'll need a little bit of speed to slide the clubhead through all of that grass, so make sure to complete your swing. Your follow-through should be at least as long as your backswing.

What if... The ball is perched atop the grass, and you have a reasonable amount of green to work with?

If the ball sits atop the grass like a scoop of vanilla ice cream in a cone, be careful not to sole the club down in the grass, because this could cause the ball to move. Other than that, there's really not much danger to this shot. In fact, I think it's much easier than people make it out to be.

Grip down to the metal on the shaft and hover the clubhead so that the leading edge is level with the bottom of the ball (see FIGURE 3.30). Make a very smooth swing with very little wrist action, almost as if you're hitting a long chip. Obviously, the longer the shot, the more wrist cock you'll need, but you want to feel as if you're sweeping the ball off the top of the grass. The ball should pop out like a normal pitch shot, with a high-enough trajectory to carry onto the putting surface.

3.30

Escape from Tall Grass from 90 Yards

Your second shot on the par 5 sails wildly off to the right into a field of deep fescue grass. After a search of a few minutes, you find your ball in the hay, about 90 yards from the green. It's going to take a mighty lash to get the ball on the green, so here's how to give yourself a reasonable chance at a par.

There are actually two ways you can play this shot. If you need a lot of height (that is, it's all carry to the green), then you have to play it like a cut shot, swinging the club along your shoulder line but across your target line. If the fairway is firm and there's a lot of runway between you and the hole, then chase the ball up onto the green using the sledgehammer method prescribed further on (see page 72). Here are my keys to pulling off both shots.

MARTIN'S KEYS FOR THE HIGH FESCUE SHOT

- Play the ball slightly forward of center in your stance, with your feet, hips, and shoulders aimed well left of the target and the clubface open to your stance line.

- Hang on tight with both hands (a grip pressure of 11, on a scale from 1–10) to prevent the clubhead from turning over and getting hung up in the grass. Ankle-deep fescue has a tendency to wrap around the hosel and shut the clubface down, so you need to increase your grip pressure to keep the face from closing.

- Swing the club down along your shoulder line on a very steep out-to-in path. Notice how low Seve's right shoulder is, an indication of how steep his shoulder plane is and how well he's stayed behind the ball (see FIGURE 3.31). You want to keep your head and upper body behind the ball, which creates height.

3.31

MARTIN'S KEYS FOR THE LOW FESCUE SHOT

- Play the ball back in your stance with most of your weight on your forward foot. Your clubface and shoulders should be square to the target line, not open.

- Envision a sharp angle down into the ball, and swing the club on the very same angle. Pick the club more or less straight up in the air and chop down on the ball as if you were using the clubhead like a sledgehammer, smashing into concrete.
- Keep your weight steady on your front foot throughout the swing. The ball should come out low and tumble forward with very little backspin and plenty of forward roll.

4

Great Sand Escapes

While most boys his age went to the beach to build sand castles and frolic around in the water, Seve Ballesteros carved divots in the sand. He carried with him an old wooden-shafted 3-iron and learned how to slip it underneath the ball and make it do all kinds of wonderful things. As a result, he was able to hit bunker shots with a 3-iron as well as most professionals could with a sand iron. He developed the hand-eye coordination to hit the correct amount of sand he wanted to, with a lot of speed, so that he could spin the ball when needed.

You'll often hear professional golfers talk about how they'd prefer playing from a greenside bunker than pitching from the rough, and the reason for that is their ability to spin the ball. It's much easier to hit the ball high and spin it out of a bunker, because you can control how much sand you take—the less you take, the more you spin it (although you do have to take some sand). In the greenside rough, you can steepen your angle of attack, but you're still going to catch a fair amount of grass between the ball and the clubface, which reduces spin.

In this chapter, I'll show you exactly how Seve was able to use this spin to his advantage to hit all sorts of bunker shots. I'll also teach you how to create some fizz of your own, so that you're not anxious the next time you're faced with a high lip or short pin location. Not all bunker shots draw a nice lie in the sand, either, so I've included some basic instructions on how to escape from a buried lie and a few uneven ones as well.

There's no reason why a trip to the greenside bunker can't feel like a day at the beach again, and it should be no cause for concern, provided you make the right setup adjustments and learn how to use the loft of the club correctly. Here's how.

Cut Bunker Shot

One way to stop the ball relatively fast out of the sand is to throw it high up in the air, with cutspin. Because of the left-to-right spin, the ball will land softly on the green with some sideways movement, instead of releasing forward with a lot of topspin and perhaps even running off the green. It's the ideal shot when you need to stop the ball quickly, or when the green is running away from you.

The technique used for the cut bunker shot is very similar to that of a standard greenside bunker shot, except that some higher-skilled players will try to contact the sand very close to the ball to generate extra spin—this puts you in danger of hitting the shot thin, and is not something I'd recommend for most recreational golfers. In the pictures here, you can see that Seve sets up with his hands about even with the ball and his head clearly behind the ball (see FIGURE 4.1). I like the idea of setting up with your head back because it encourages you to hit the sand first, "south of the border," as I like to say. The sand is what moves the ball up and out of the bunker, and if you hit the ball first, you're going to hit the aforementioned rocket ball shot.

4.1

4.2

At impact, Seve's lower body has slid forward just a little bit (which is how he makes contact so close to the ball), but his head and upper body remain behind the ball, where they were at address. His right shoulder is working down and under his chin, which helps him slide the clubhead under the ball and propel it out of the bunker (see FIGURE 4.2). The cutspin is created by his setup, because the clubface is open relative to the path of his swing, causing the ball to cut slightly from left to right.

MARTIN'S KEYS

- Set up with your shoulders and hips pointing left of the target and the clubface pointing at the target, while remembering that the target isn't always the flagstick. The ball should be just forward of center in your stance, with your head back behind the ball to assist you in contacting the sand first.

- Kick your right knee in and flare both feet out 45 degrees to add stability and help brace the lower body as you swing back. Make a three-quarter-length backswing, cocking your wrists to help you generate more clubhead speed through impact. You need speed to spin the ball.

- Swing the club down on the same plane your shoulders are on at address, cutting across the target line from out to in, just as if you were hitting a cutspin shot in tennis. Imagine that the ball sits on a tee, and try to knock the tee out from under the ball as you swing through into a full finish position. The higher the shot, the higher you need to finish (see FIGURE 4.3). Keep the right shoulder down as you swing through; you don't want this shoulder coming up, because that all but guarantees thin contact.

4.3

Divots: Cup of Tea, Soup, or Dinner?

One way to vary the distance of your bunker shots without changing the speed or length of your swing is by controlling the depth of the divot you take. Given a consistent length and speed of swing, the shallower the divot, the farther the ball will travel, and vice versa. For short bunker shots, I recommend carving out a divot the depth of a teacup in the sand (in other words, fairly deep); for medium-length bunker shots, a soup bowl or a dessert dish; and for longer bunker shots, a dinner plate (see FIGURE 4.4). Regardless of the amount of sand you take, the deepest part of the divot should always be under the ball. This is an indication that the clubhead is entering the sand behind the ball and exiting on the target side of the ball.

If the sand is hard and firm, try to hit the ball a little softer—that is, swing shorter and slower. But if it's fluffy and very soft, take a full swing and hit the sand harder, because you'll have to move lots of it to get the ball on the green. It's easier to spin the ball from hard sand because less of it gets trapped between the clubface and the ball.

Tea   Soup   Dinner

4.4

What if... The ball rests close to the face of the bunker and you have to pop it up extremely fast?

If there's one shot I mastered while growing up in England, it was this one. I certainly had a lot of practice at it, having encountered more than my fair share of pot bunkers along the way. When you're staring at the face of a bunker, and you've got to make the ball rise almost straight up in the air, you can't be afraid to take some sand. You need to throw the clubhead under the ball with your right hand, just as if you were holding a tub of ice cream in your left hand and scooping it out with your right (see FIGURE 4.5). The ball will shoot out higher than your normal bunker shot and will land very softly.

To execute the "spoon" shot, play the ball slightly forward of center in your stance, with your weight favoring your front leg. Allow your upper body to fall into a slight reverse tilt as you swing

(CONTINUED)

4.5

(CONTINUED)

down, so that your spine leans marginally away from the target at impact and your head is behind the ball. This will help you throw the clubhead under the ball. Try to get the sweet spot of the clubface directly under the ball and knock the sand out from under it. Your right palm should point to the sky shortly after impact, as this photo of Seve bears out (see FIGURE 4.6), which is indicative of the scooping action that takes place under the ball.

4.6

High-Spinning Bunker Shot

The long bunker shot is notorious for being one of the hardest shots in golf, but the short bunker shot to a close pin location is no picnic, either. To get this shot reasonably close, you need to generate a lot of clubhead speed and spin. One way to get both is to grip down to the metal on the shaft, as Seve is doing here (see FIGURE 4.7). By holding onto the thinnest part of the golf club, your hands will be more active through the swing, helping you slide the clubface under the ball more easily and increase the effective loft on the club. Gripping down effectively gives you a shorter club, allowing you to swing faster and hit the ball a shorter distance.

By gripping down so far on the club and creating such a short lever, Seve's hands are very low to the ground. He's also standing farther away from the ball, which, combined with the low-hands position, helps him put more loft on the club. His backswing is very short (see FIGURE 4.8), which allows him to go after the ball with quite a bit of gusto. Seve makes a very wristy swing without a lot of arm movement. The wrists are capable of generating a tremendous amount of speed, and Seve puts them to good use in this swing, as evidenced by how quickly he's rehinged the wrists after impact (see FIGURE 4.9).

This is a very high-risk shot because you have to be wristy and generate a lot of speed with a very short swing, but by gripping down to the shaft you can afford to be aggressive and, who knows, you may stop the ball right next to the pin.

MARTIN'S KEYS

- Play the ball just forward of center in your stance, which should be slightly wider than normal, or outside shoulder-width. Grip down to the steel portion of the shaft and bend forward from the hips to allow for this; otherwise you might hit the shot thin.

- Pick the club up fairly steeply on the backswing, and slide the clubhead underneath the ball with a lot of zip, just as if you were striking a match (see FIGURE 4.10). You should carve out a very thin layer of sand between the ball and the clubface.

- As you swing through, unhinge and rehinge your wrists very quickly. You'll create tremendous speed and friction between the sand, the ball, and the clubface, imparting extra spin on the ball so that it can land softly on the green

4.10

What if... The ball is buried in the sand and you're hitting to a short pin?

Forget the hole location: The goal is to get the ball anywhere on the green; even the fringe isn't a bad result. If the ball is fully submerged in the sand and you can't get the clubhead under the ball, you can't spin it. Nobody can. You've got to essentially dig the ball out and hope for the best.

There are two ways you can play this shot: (1) You can put the ball back in your stance and chop down hard into the sand with a slightly open clubface; or (2) you can turn the face in 45 degrees (see FIGURE 4.11) so that the sharp toe end of the club cuts through the sand like a bayonet knifing its way into a sandbag. I learned this "bayonet" method from former European Ryder Cupper Tom Haliburton, who was my boss at the Wentworth Club. If you turn the face in, you don't have to swing as hard to get the club through the sand as you do with a square or an open clubface. You play the ball back in your stance and try to hook it ever so slightly, swinging a bit to the right of the target line through impact. The "bayonet" shoots a tsunami wave of sand forward, which pushes the ball out of the bunker (see FIGURE 4.12). A word of warning: The ball will come out relatively low with a lot of roll, so do not attempt this shot if the lip of the bunker is more than a few feet high.

4.11

4.12

with some extra bite. Gary Player, one of the best bunker players in the history of the game and a great influence on Seve, uses the image of briskly striking a match to describe the action of the clubface through the sand.

Long Bunker Shot

Few shots in golf elicit more fear than a long bunker shot of 30 or more yards. Most recreational golfers have no idea how to play this shot. Afraid to skull the ball over the green or catch it heavy and leave it in the bunker, most quit at the ball, which only encourages both misses. The other critical mistake they make is using their lob or sand wedge, which, if they're going to take some sand, requires a higher amount of clubhead speed than the typical greenside bunker shot. A less lofted club, such as a 9- or an 8-iron, doesn't demand as much speed and makes the distance more manageable.

In these pictures, Seve isn't taking much sand (see FIGURES 4.13 and 4.14). He's trying to contact the sand as close to the ball as possible, which is how you maximize spin. This takes an enormous amount of skill and great hand-eye coordination, which is why I recommend that the average golfer take slightly more sand on this shot and use a lesser-lofted club. Unless you can consistently deliver the clubhead in the same precise location every time, you need the safety net that hitting an inch or two behind the ball gives you.

Seve was a big advocate of sliding the knees toward the target and keeping the head behind the ball on most short-game shots, because both movements help shallow out the club coming into the ball. If you allow your head to get in front of the ball, then you'll produce more of a downward thump into the sand, which is what you don't want on a long

4.13

4.14

bunker shot. Much of his technique can be traced back to his formative years on the beach in Spain, because the only way to loft a 3-iron gently into the air from a sandy lie is to stay behind the ball and skim the clubhead underneath it.

What if... The ball is buried, and you've got 25 to 35 yards to pin?

If you've ever skipped a rock across a pond, then you have what it takes to hit this shot. Think of it as a miniature hook shot with a 9-iron, similar to the St. Andrew's Runner in chapter 2 (pages 32–33). Play the ball back in your stance, with your feet, hips, and shoulders aimed right of your target, and the clubface closed just slightly. Swing the clubhead more to the inside and around your body going back, stopping when your hands are at about 9 o'clock (see FIGURE 4.15). As you swing through, have the feeling that your right palm is turning down toward the ground and the club is swinging down the target line, one of the rare times that it will (see FIGURE 4.16). This helps you close the face and impart hookspin on the ball.

This is one shot where you're not thinking about getting the deepest part of the divot directly under the ball; instead, you want to throw the ball forward and have it ride out on a wave of sand. The more sand you take, the harder it's going to be to move the ball the required distance.

4.15   4.16

MARTIN'S KEYS

- Play this as you would a normal greenside bunker shot, only with an 8- or a 9-iron and not your sand wedge. Open the clubface slightly to expose more of the club's bounce, which helps the clubhead glide through the sand versus dig into it. Your weight should be evenly distributed on both feet (about 50–50), and the ball positioned forward of center in your stance to ensure that you catch the sand first.

- Aim your feet and shoulders left of the target, and swing along your shoulder line, cutting across the target line just slightly. Try to splash the sand out from under the ball, propelling it toward the green. You don't want to hit a hand grenade–type shot, where the sand flies straight up in the air; the sand has to move straight forward, because the ball has such a great distance to travel.

- Make a three-quarter swing back and through at your normal speed (see FIGURE 4.17), because the reduced loft will more than make up for the extra yardage.

4.17

Ball above Your Feet

Any time the ball is above your feet, whether you're in the sand or hitting off a fairway lie, the ball is going to go left. This is especially true with a lofted club, such as a sand wedge, because the more you flatten the shaft angle, the more the face effectively points left. Therefore, the first thing to do when playing this shot is to aim your body and club to the right of the flagstick, as Seve is doing here (see FIGURE 4.18). You should also stand a little farther away from the ball than normal to encourage a shallower swing path on both the backswing and downswing.

As for the swing itself, you can see that Seve's shoulders rotate on a fairly level plane throughout the shot (see FIGURES 4.19 and 4.20). The fatal flaw amateurs make is that they swing their right shoulder down on too steep an angle—too far under their chin—which causes them to take too much of a divot and hit the shot heavy. To combat this, stand taller at

address so that your upper body is almost erect. This will help you swing flatter, both back and through, on a more horizontal plane.

Also, note how Seve's right shoulder rotates toward his chosen target, several yards right of the flagstick and not toward the flagstick itself (see FIGURE 4.21). This is very important because many amateurs try to steer the ball toward the flagstick, which sets up a steep out-to-in motion and not the flatter angle you need with this swing. Think about rotating your shoulders level to the ground going back and through, and swing to your target. If you do this, you should take a relatively thin divot and pop the ball up and out of the bunker very gently.

What if… The ball is half-buried under the lip of the bunker?

You cannot do the impossible, so make sure that the height of the lip and the position of the ball will allow you to attempt the shot. You can't make the ball go straight up in the air, so there has to be some space between the ball and the lip of the bunker in order to get it out. Set up with your spine perpendicular to the slope and the ball position favoring your front foot. Pick the club up very steeply, and then slam the clubhead down into the sand, driving the clubhead underneath the ball (see FIGURE 4.22).

Here's where it gets interesting: As soon as you feel the clubhead reaching the bottom of its arc, back it up as if you were throwing your vehicle into reverse (see FIGURE 4.23). Stop when you get to the end of your backswing position (see FIGURE 4.24). The ball should ride out on a pillow of sand, due to the downward nature of the blow. The reason this "bang and recoil" method works so well is that by immediately pulling the club back, you don't throw

4.22

as much sand over the top of the ball. If you drown the ball with too much sand, it's not going to get the height it needs to clear the lip of the bunker.

4.23

4.24

MARTIN'S KEYS

- Stand a little farther away from the ball than normal and add some flex to your knees so that your upper body is virtually erect. This will help you swing your arms on a much more horizontal plane, which is necessary when the ball is sitting above your feet.

What if... The ball settles under the back lip of the bunker?

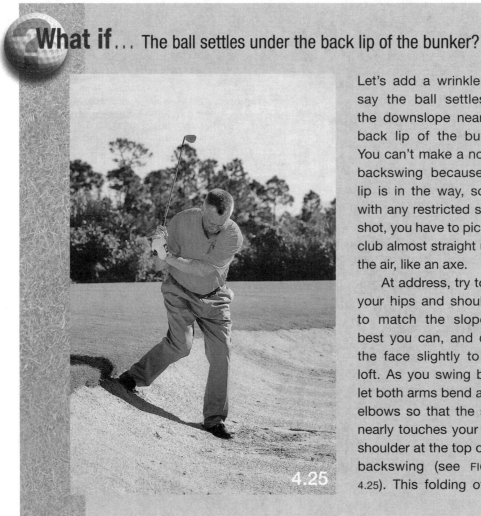
4.25

Let's add a wrinkle and say the ball settles on the downslope near the back lip of the bunker. You can't make a normal backswing because the lip is in the way, so, as with any restricted swing shot, you have to pick the club almost straight up in the air, like an axe.

At address, try to get your hips and shoulders to match the slope as best you can, and open the face slightly to add loft. As you swing back, let both arms bend at the elbows so that the shaft nearly touches your right shoulder at the top of the backswing (see FIGURE 4.25). This folding of the

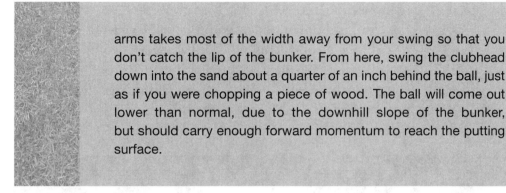

arms takes most of the width away from your swing so that you don't catch the lip of the bunker. From here, swing the clubhead down into the sand about a quarter of an inch behind the ball, just as if you were chopping a piece of wood. The ball will come out lower than normal, due to the downhill slope of the bunker, but should carry enough forward momentum to reach the putting surface.

- Aim your body and clubface several yards to the right of the flagstick to account for the face pointing left.
- Have a sense that your shoulders are swinging level to the ground, both back and through, and swing toward your "chosen" target, not toward the flagstick.

Ball below Your Feet

Whereas the ball above your feet is closer to your body, this one is farther away. As a result, you have to bend forward more than usual in order to get the clubhead underneath the ball. The more inclined your upper body is, the steeper the plane of your swing is going to be, and the more likely you are to impart some cutspin (left-to-right movement) on the ball. Consequently, you'll want to aim your body left of the flagstick to allow the ball to cut back toward the hole.

In this set of pictures, Seve's upper torso is almost parallel to the ground and his knees are flexed considerably, which helps with balance and, equally as important, assists in getting the clubhead down underneath the ball (see FIGURES 4.26 and 4.27). Once he starts his swing, Seve does a wonderful job of maintaining his balance and staying down through the entire shot, which allows him to loft the ball out gently onto the putting surface (see FIGURES 4.28 and 4.29).

4.26

4.27

MARTIN'S KEYS

- Widen your stance and put more weight on your heels to help counterbalance your upper body being bent over so much (in other words, closer to the ground).

- On the backswing, pick up your arms steeply, as if you were swinging an axe, and then throw the clubhead directly

What if... You face a downhill bunker shot, and the green is sloping away from you?

Although balance is crucial, the bigger issue facing you is how to get the ball to stop once it lands on the green. As with any downhill lie, it's going to be extremely difficult to create extra height on the shot, so your only real chance of stopping the ball is to put a lot of cutspin on it, similar to a one-handed slice backhand shot in tennis.

4.30

At address, open the clubface slightly, aim your body left of the target, and match your hips and shoulders to the slope. Lean with the slope as well. Most golfers' natural inclination is to lean backward, because it's more comfortable and easier to maintain your balance that way, but your weight has to be moving forward, down the slope, through impact. On the backswing, fan the face open a bit to create some additional loft and spin. From there, have the feeling that you're chasing the clubhead down the slope, with lots of speed. Keep the knuckles on your right hand pointing to the ground for as long as you can, as you blast the sand out from underneath the ball (see FIGURE 4.30). Your hands should swing around your left hip into the finish, which helps keep the face pointing to the sky. The ball should still come off fairly low—more of a medium trajectory—but with a tremendous amount of cutspin on it, providing for a softer landing.

underneath the ball. Your right shoulder should move down under your chin and then rotate toward your target.

- Think about maintaining the flex in both knees and keeping your chest pointed down at the ground throughout the entire swing. As you finish, let your head rotate as if you were laying your right ear on an imaginary pillow. This helps you stay in your original address posture so that you don't come up out of the shot too early and hit a rocket ball over the green.

Left Foot Out, Right Foot In

Sometimes the ball comes to rest so close to the lip or the bottom face of the bunker that you're restricted from taking your normal stance. In the photo here (see FIGURE 4.31), you can see that Seve's left foot is completely out of the sand and resting on the grass face of the bunker. Yet by anchoring his foot there and bending his left knee substantially, he's still able to get his spine perpendicular to the slope and his hips and shoulders parallel to the slope. Now it's just a matter of using the cock-and-pop method from earlier (see "ball half-buried under the lip of the bunker" on pages 90–91), minus the recoil.

4.31

MARTIN'S KEYS

- Because the ball is on an upslope, you need to alter your stance in such a way that your body is nearly parallel to the slope, and your feet are well anchored to the ground. Balance is essential to any bunker shot, especially one from a challenging lie such as this, because the more your body moves around, the harder it is to bottom the club out in the right spot.

- Pick the club up sharply on the backswing, cocking both wrists fully. Throw the clubhead hard into the face of the bunker, just underneath the ball (SEE FIGURE 4.32). Even though the bunker face acts like a brick wall, stopping the advance of your club, you still want to feel as if the deepest part of the divot is under the ball.

- Be mindful of your balance, keeping your head very still as you swing back and through.

4.32

Long, Short, and Breaking Putts

Y ou might be wondering what's "Houdini-like" about sinking a putt. But sometimes, holing an 8-foot left-to-right breaking putt for par can be as miraculous as holing out from a greenside bunker or as exhilarating as executing a well-placed lob shot. And if you've ever faced a 3-foot downhill putt with a tournament or a match on the line, you know it's not as easy as the shortness of the shot might suggest. Some of the most memorable shots in golf have been putts—Constantino Rocca's 100-foot putt from the "Valley of Sin" at the 1995 Open Championship; Tiger Woods's 15-foot birdie putt on the 72nd hole of the

2008 U.S. Open to force a playoff with Rocco Mediate; Justin Leonard's 40-foot bomb to cap off a dramatic U.S. comeback at the 1999 Ryder Cup; Jack Nicklaus's 18-foot birdie putt ("Yes, sir") on the 71st hole at the 1986 Masters to highlight a brilliant back-nine charge at age forty-six. And while he'll be remembered most for his tremendous shotmaking skills around the green, it's his jubilant celebration following a birdie putt on the final hole of the 1984 British Open at St. Andrew's that will stand as the enduring image of Seve Ballesteros. For the longest time, the ball hung on the edge of the hole before dropping in for the clinching birdie—perhaps even being kicked in by the ghost of Old Tom Morris. A giddy Seve swung his right arm across his chest, let out a big scream of delight, and then pumped his right fist several times before walking off the green with his arm around his caddie.

It's been said that a hot putter can make up for a lot of sins, and never has there been a truer statement. It's your "get out of jail free" card. You can pop your drive up, chunk the next two shots, and still walk away very pleased with yourself after holing a 30-footer for par. Or you can curse yourself up and down for leaving your pitch shot on the wrong side of the hole, then drop a slippery 12-footer for your par, and strut away as if you had planned it that way all along.

There are elements of shotmaking and strategy in putting, too, just as there are in chipping, pitching, and bunker play. Here are a few putts, from the 3-foot knee-knocker to the difficult left-to-right breaker, that will test your nerves and your touch.

Long Lag Putt

Seve definitely had his own unique style of putting. His arms were fairly bent, his hands low, and his right index finger was somewhat extended down the grip. I was always under the impression that I was watching a surgeon holding a scalpel, about to operate. He also used some wrists in his putting stroke, which is clearly evident in these photos (see FIGURES 5.1 and 5.2).

The longer the putt—for example, 30 feet or more—the more advisable it is to hinge your wrists some on the backswing. Why? Because they're a source of power in your stroke. The biggest mistake the typical club player makes is to take too short a backswing, with little to no wrists, and then try to

5.1

5.2

put all of the power into the stroke on the through-swing. The result is usually a mis-hit and a putt that comes up several feet or more short of the hole—or way past the hole. When you don't hinge your wrists, then you have only one lever and one speed producer—the arms and shoulders—to generate power. The only way to get the ball to the hole, then, is to make an especially long backswing or overaccelerate the hands and arms through impact. By hinging the wrists, however, you create an additional second lever, and more power, so you don't have to swing as much. This allows you to make a smooth transition into the forward stroke and hit the ball more solidly, making it easier to gauge distance.

In Seve's lag putting stroke, there's some give in the left wrist through impact, and his right wrist has lost most of its angle. The toe of the putter has passed the heel and is a foot or more off the ground. This is important to note because many golfers artificially try to keep the putterhead low to the ground after impact, which restricts the face from closing and squaring to the putt's starting line. In a good putting stroke, the putter swings naturally, like a pendulum, and arcs upward after impact.

Not only does the putterhead swing on an up-and-down arc, but it also swings in (on the backstroke) to in (on the throughstroke), relative to the target line. It does not move straight back and straight through. As with your other clubs, the shaft attaches to the head at an angle, so it has to swing on an arc. You can have the feeling that the putterhead is moving straight back and straight through, but on a putt of 30 feet or more, you have to let the putterhead swing in to in. Anything else would be unnatural and would make it more difficult to control the speed and distance of the putt.

MARTIN'S KEYS

- Take two or three practice strokes about 2 feet behind the ball, on an extension of the putt's starting line (see FIGURE

5.3). Look at the hole as you take your rehearsal swings to get a better feel for the distance and the amount of stroke you need to get the ball to the hole. I've found that this helps players reach the hole more often, instead of leaving putts short. Research says the optimal speed for making

5.3

most putts has the ball rolling about 18 inches (nearly 2 feet) past the hole, if it doesn't go in. Taking your practice swing a little farther from the hole helps you do just that.

- Make sure there's a good rhythm to your practice strokes. Try saying "one thousand" on your backswing, and "one" to impact. When you're finished, move right in and assume your setup, with the ball just forward of center in your stance.

- Let the putter swing, hinging your wrists slightly going back to create some additional speed in your stroke. If the putt is really long, allow your legs to move a little to provide even more power.

Short Knee-Knocker (3–4 feet)

During many casual rounds of golf, you rarely have to putt out from 3 feet—your playing partners just give it to you. So when you absolutely have to make them (in a tournament, in a match-play situation, or when money's at stake, and so on), it's little wonder your skin gets all clammy and your hands and knees start to tremble. That's why they call these putts *knee-knockers*—they're short enough that you expect to make them 100 percent of the time, but just long enough to create some anxiety. And the more you miss them, the more they get in your head. The fact is, these are anything but gimmes under even the most normal of situations. Most 3-footers have some break to them, but not usually outside the hole, and it's easy to underestimate the difficulty of getting the line and the speed correct.

Throughout his career, Seve was terrific at holing putts when it mattered the most. One reason for this, I'm sure, is that he gave every 3- and 4-foot putt a tremendous amount of respect. You can see this in his technique: He kept both arms fairly close to his body throughout the stroke, which enhanced his chances of hitting the ball with a square putterface. He was also careful not to alter his address posture during the stroke. Many golfers lift their heads just prior to impact, which opens the shoulders and makes square contact extremely difficult. Seve's head swiveled toward the target as if it were an apple on a stick (see FIGURE 5.4); it did not come up one inch until the ball was well on its way.

5.4

On most short putts, there's not a lot of break. Rarely will you have to aim outside the hole. Direction is more important than speed; therefore, the angle of the clubface at impact is vital to start the ball on line. And if you start the ball on-line, your chances of holing the putt are very good. (This doesn't mean that speed is irrelevant.)

What if... You're left with a fairly quick, downhill 3- to 4-foot breaking putt?

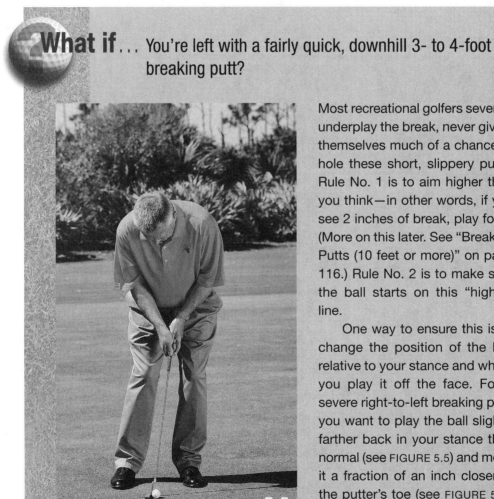

5.5

Most recreational golfers severely underplay the break, never giving themselves much of a chance to hole these short, slippery putts. Rule No. 1 is to aim higher than you think—in other words, if you see 2 inches of break, play for 4. (More on this later. See "Breaking Putts (10 feet or more)" on page 116.) Rule No. 2 is to make sure the ball starts on this "higher" line.

One way to ensure this is to change the position of the ball relative to your stance and where you play it off the face. For a severe right-to-left breaking putt, you want to play the ball slightly farther back in your stance than normal (see FIGURE 5.5) and move it a fraction of an inch closer to the putter's toe (see FIGURE 5.6). It also helps to put more weight on your front foot so that you're more likely to have your body ahead of the ball at impact. All of these things promote a slightly open putterface at impact, so that the ball automatically starts to the right of the hole, on the high side.

If you have a severe left-to-right breaking putt, then do just the opposite: play the ball farther forward in your stance (closer to your left foot) and move it fractionally closer to the heel of the putter. This promotes a slightly closed face position at impact, so that the putt automatically starts to the left of the hole. To further encourage the release of the putterhead, feel as if you're swinging the putter with just your right hand only. Find a couple of short breaking putts on the practice green that bend in both directions, and practice each making the setup adjustments described above. Once you learn to get the ball off high enough, you'll see a lot more putts start to drop.

5.6

MARTIN'S KEYS

- One way that some people have success is to bend both thumbs so that the fingernails make contact with the top, flat portion of the grip (see FIGURE 5.7). This helps keep the

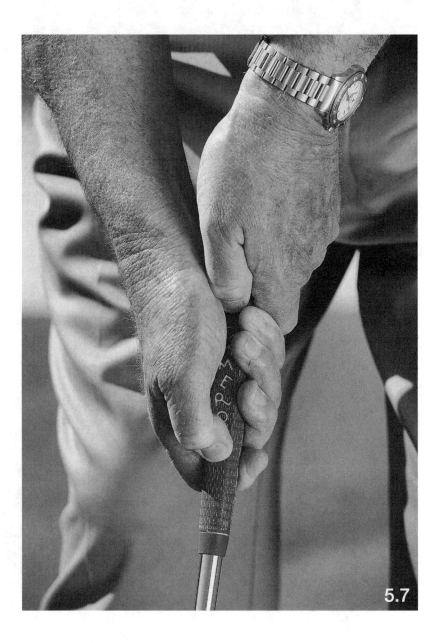

5.7

wrists very quiet through the stroke, so the putter has a better chance of hitting the ball with a square face. If you can consistently get the face square to the putt's starting line, you're going to make the vast majority of your 3-footers.

- Make a very short stroke with not much follow-through, allowing the putterhead to come to a quiet stop after impact (in other words, no wobbling). The image I like to give golfers is one of driving a tack into the back of a ball—it's a short pop, with no deliberate or conscious follow-through (see FIGURE 5.8). This image helps you accelerate the clubhead into the ball, much like a hammer into a nail, and deliver a firm hit.

- Keep your lower body motionless during the entire stroke, because the slightest wobble in your lower body can cause the putterface to open or close.

5.8

Extremely Fast Downhill Putts

You find yourself 15 feet above the hole, staring at a downhill, downgrain putt so fast that all you have to do is breathe the ball's way and it will start rolling. It's going to be next to impossible to leave it short of the hole, but if you're not careful, you may have a much longer putt coming back.

The best players in the world recognize when the putt is downgrain (in other words, there's a shiny texture to the grass), so they know to be gentle and contact the ball as if they were hitting it with their shadow. Most amateurs, however, tend to underestimate the speed and give no consideration to grain. They don't assess the conditions carefully enough to know just how extreme the slope is. When you're walking up to the green to mark your ball, you need to take in as much information as you can about the slope of the green, the direction of the wind, and the firmness of the green. Then, as you're reading the putt, look to see if there's a shiny glare to the grass between you and the hole. If there is, you're putting downgrain and the putt will be extremely quick; if it's dull or darker in appearance, then you're putting into the grain and you can expect the roll to be somewhat slower. All of these things will give you a clue as to the severity of the slope and the speed of the putt.

If there are two things you should take away from the photo of Seve here (see FIGURE 5.9), it's how his eyes are directly over the line of the putt and the putterhead is up off the ground after impact. It doesn't stay low to the ground, and it doesn't stop the instant it contacts the ball. There's some acceleration through the ball, albeit very gentle, and the putter is traveling on an arc, very similar to how a pendulum swings.

Almost all golfers, when faced with this situation, hit the ball too hard. They make insufficient allowance for both the slope and the grain and what these will do to the ball. What

you want to do is swing the putterhead through the ball at the
same slow, deliberate pace you took it back on. You don't want
to add any extra acceleration to the putterhead; you want it to
move on the same smooth, even pace back and through.

MARTIN'S KEYS

- Foreshorten the hole in your mind's eye. In other words, pretend there's a second hole several feet closer to you (depending on the speed of the putt), and putt to this imaginary hole.

- As you examine the line of the putt, rotate your head down the line at approximately the same speed you want the ball to roll (see FIGURES 5.10 and 5.11). This helps set the speed for the stroke. On really fast, slick downhill putts, you want to rotate the head very slowly.

5.10

5.11

- Imagine that the putter shaft is made of very delicate glass—similar to the thin stem of a champagne glass—and swing it back and through very slowly without shattering the glass. You want to contact the ball lightly, as if you're stroking a dog, just to get the ball in motion. Do not tap the ball as if you were hammering a nail, because that will break the glass and send the ball scooting past the hole.

- Another way to take speed off the ball is to hit it very slightly toward the toe of the putter, as we discussed earlier with the short, downhill breaking putt (see page 108). If you mis-hit it on purpose, you're not going to get the full energy on the ball. It would be like hitting the ball with the headcover still on your putter.

- As a drill to help you groove this ultra-smooth stroke, stick a coin on the back cavity of your putter (assuming there is a cavity) and make several practice swings without losing the coin (see FIG-URES 5.12 and 5.13). There can be no sudden acceleration or jerking of the putterhead or the coin will fall off. The transition also has to be very smooth and the head has to glide into the finish.

Breaking Putts (10 feet or more)

The pull of gravity is ever-present in our world. The second someone fires an arrow up into the sky, gravity tries to knock it back down to earth. And it succeeds. In a matter of seconds, the arrow reaches its highest point and then starts arcing toward the ground. The point at which the arrow is farthest from the ground is not where the archer actually aims the arrow, however—it's significantly lower. That's the effect gravity has on the arrow. If a marksman is shooting at a target 800 yards away, he's not going to aim straight at the target; rather, he's going to aim slightly above the target and allow for the pull of gravity to bring the bullet back down to earth. (He also has to factor in the wind.)

The point I'm trying to make is that when you have a significant amount of break to a putt, you don't aim the putterhead at the apex, or high point, of the putt, as most traditional instruction suggests. You aim at a point higher than the apex, because the second the ball leaves your putter, it starts to get pulled off its intended path, due to gravity. Think of it another way: if you're hitting your approach shot into a 50 mph right-to-left wind, and you aim 30 yards right of the flagstick to allow for the wind, the instant you hit the ball the wind starts to move it to the left. That's what happens on a breaking putt; it's just that gravity, created by the slope of the green, is acting like the wind. If you start it at the apex, the putt will miss on the low side of the hole. Guaranteed!

In the photo of Seve here, you can clearly see that his feet and shoulders are aimed higher than the actual apex of the putt (see FIGURE 5.14). In the case of the left-to-right breaking putt, he's aimed a good foot or more left of the putt's apex. He's stroking the putt as if it were a straight putt, to a target well left of the hole, but he's letting the slope and gravity pull the ball toward the hole. His putter is swinging in the same general direction where he's aimed, *above* the apex of the putt's roll.

5.14

MARTIN'S KEYS

- Take a good look at the putt from behind the ball, then walk to the hole and back along the low side of the putt to get a better sense of how much slope and break there are.

- Determine where the apex, or high point, of the putt's roll is going to be, and then aim the putterface at a point several inches or more higher than the apex (represented by the water bottle in this picture; see FIGURE 5.15). This is your

5.15

putt's true aiming point. The more severe the break is, the higher this point becomes.

- Settle your eyes over the putt's starting line, and make your normal stroke, swinging in the direction of your true aiming point (see FIGURE 5.16). Imagine that there's a straight line between the ball and this point, and that's where you want it to go. The pull of gravity and the slope will move the ball toward the hole.

5.16

6

Various Other Houdini-like Escapes

Billy Foster, Seve Ballesteros's caddie of five years (from 1990 to '95), had a front-row seat for many of the Spaniard's greatest escapes, including one particular Houdini-like shot at the 1993 European Masters in Switzerland. After leaving his tee shot directly behind an 8-foot-high swimming pool wall, Seve managed to hit a 150-yard wedge over the wall to 15 feet short of the green, evading some overhanging branches along the way. He then proceeded to chip in for birdie.

Foster, who has caddied for the likes of Darren Clarke, Thomas Bjorn, Sergio Garcia, and Lee Westwood since then, says it remains the greatest shot he's ever seen.

"I was saying, 'I know you're Seve Ballesteros, but you're not a magician, just chip it out sideways.' And he said, 'Don't worry, Billy—this shot is no problem,'" Foster recalled shortly after Ballesteros's death in 2011. "He waved me away and proceeded to hit a wedge with half a backswing over the wall, through some trees where there was a tiny gap the size of a dinner plate, over a swimming pool, and got it 5 yards short of the green.

"Seve just laughed, and I got down on my hands and knees and bowed to him."

It wasn't the first time Ballesteros brought a caddie, a fellow player, or a casual observer to his knees with a miraculous recovery shot. Hale Irwin was playing alongside Ballesteros in the final group at the 1979 Open Championship when Seve famously hit his tee shot into a parking lot on the course adjacent to the 16th fairway at Royal Lytham & St. Anne's. Seve went on to make birdie and win the first of his five major championships.

"I'm leading, and I watched the guy hit three fairways all day and win the British Open," said Irwin. "It wasn't because he was lucky, it was because he created some shots that were unbelievable."

Seve's determination to fight for every single stroke, no matter how big a hole he put himself in, was on full display during the 1995 Ryder Cup Matches in Rochester, New York. Playing singles against Tom Lehman in his eighth and final Ryder Cup appearance, Ballesteros hit the ball all over Western New York. He didn't hit a single fairway on the front nine, often finding himself in the woods, yet managed to string together one miraculous par after another to keep the match close. Lehman eventually beat Ballesteros 4 and 3, but any other player would've lost 9 and 8, considering the places Seve was hitting from. His resoluteness that day, even when his game had left him, was infectious, and inspired the Europeans to a dramatic comeback win over the heavily favored Americans.

In this chapter, I'll take a look at some of Seve's most improbable escapes, and explain how he was able to make the ball curve around trees and fly over or under them when necessary. I'll teach you how to play shots off a variety of different surfaces—half grass, half sand; hardpan; pine straw—and even how to hit a ball off your knees. Yes, your knees. As Seve proved throughout his playing career, if you have a swing, a good imagination, and a strong willingness to succeed, you have a chance. Not every shot in golf is going to find a piece of lush fairway grass. The more prepared you are for the unordinary circumstance, the more likely you are to make some miracles of your own happen with your short game.

Half Grass, Half Sand

Your approach shot comes to rest a few feet outside a greenside bunker. Feeling relief initially, you start to wonder whether you'd been better off in the sand when you encounter the lie—half grass, half sand. Before you do anything, you have to determine how much sand there is under the ball. If it's mainly sand, and there are only a few blades of grass sprinkled in, then you can aim a few inches behind the ball and play it like a normal greenside bunker shot. If it's mainly grass, however, and the ground is relatively firm, then you have to make ball-first contact. In the latter instance, it will be very difficult to stop the ball quickly; you'll want to leave yourself a little margin for error where your target is concerned.

Seve looks to have drawn a grassy lie in this picture, which would explain why so much of his body is in front of the ball

6.1

(see FIGURE 6.1). This will promote a steep angle into the ball, so that he can contact the ball more cleanly. Normally, the shot will come off low, but Seve—never one to be satisfied with just escaping trouble—has found a way to negate the low trajectory by twisting the clubface open on the backswing. (Either that or he started with a wide-open clubface at address.) Now he can hit down on the ball and still get enough loft on the shot to stop it on the green.

MARTIN'S KEYS

- First, determine how much sand there is underneath the ball. If it's mainly sand, play it like a greenside bunker shot; if it's mostly grass, play the ball back in your stance and chop it out.

- From a sandy lie, play the ball slightly forward of center in your stance, point your body left of the target, and aim the clubface at the target. Open the face a little bit more on the backswing, and try to knock the sand out from under the ball (see FIGURE 6.2). Swing to a full finish.

- From a firm, grassy lie, play the ball back in your stance with your weight favoring your front side. Set your right foot perpendicular to the target line, which will help stabilize your lower body on the backswing. Pick up the club sharply with a lot of wrist cock, and chop down on the ball. The more grass there is, the closer to the ball you want to hit.

6.2

What if... Your ball lands in a sand-filled divot, and you have only 30 to 40 yards to the pin?

The challenge here, besides making solid contact, is controlling the distance. From 120 yards away, you can assume you'll lose a few yards off your 9-iron or pitching wedge and plan accordingly, but from 30 to 40 yards away, there's no telling how the shot is going to come out. The distance can be highly unpredictable, so I would recommend playing it safe and aiming for the middle of the green every time.

As far as technique goes, you're not going to scoop the ball out of this lie (see FIGURE 6.3). It's going to require a steep downward blow and a deeper divot than usual. Contact has to be very precise, with the club bottoming out just ahead of the ball, on the target side of the ball. Set up with the ball back in your stance, just opposite the inside of your right heel, with your upper body leaning forward and hands ahead of the ball. Grip the club firmly with both hands,

6.3

6.4

and make a very short but steep backswing, hinging your wrists to create additional clubhead speed (see FIGURE 6.4). As you swing through, accelerate the clubhead down into the ground. There shouldn't be a lot of follow-through to this shot; instead, you should feel as if your entire body and the club shaft are leaning on the ball at impact.

(CONTINUED)

(CONTINUED)

In the photo of Seve here (see FIGURE 6.5), you can see just how much of his body is in front of the ball at impact. His left knee is outside his left ankle, and his nose is practically over the ball. The grip end of the shaft points to the outside of his left hip, and his right wrist remains bent, an indication of the downward nature of the blow. Seve's lower body continues to move forward through impact, which brings the low point of his swing forward, just ahead of the ball. Although you don't see it in this picture, you can bet Seve will carve out a decent-size divot on the target side of the ball.

6.5

Short Blast off Pine Needles (about 30 yards)

The hard thing about this lie is that it's like hitting a ball off a bird's nest—you have to be very careful not to slide the club straight under the ball and flub it only a few feet. You also have to be mindful not to push down on the pine needles at address, because that could move the ball. Seve, as this inset picture shows (see FIGURE 6.6), hovers the clubhead ever so slightly above the pine needles so as not to disturb them.

Seve also grips well down on the club and pulls his left foot back so that his body is fairly open to the target (see FIGURE 6.7). This promotes a steeper downswing and all but ensures he'll catch the ball first. You do not want to hit even one or two pine straws behind the ball, because that is the kiss of death. Pine straw is not brittle, like sand. Therefore, if you get any pine needles between the ball and the clubface, it deadens the impact. It's almost as if you're hitting the ball with a headcover on the club.

6.6

6.7

MARTIN'S KEYS

- Play the ball back in your stance, opposite the inside of your right heel, so that your hands are well ahead of the ball. The grip end of the club should point to the outside of your left hip. Choke down on the grip a few inches, and point your feet and shoulders left of the target line.

- Make a very slow, wrist-free backswing (pretend your wrists are in splints), and stop when your hands are at about 9 o'clock (see FIGURE 6.8).

- Start down at approximately the same speed at which you finished your backswing, so that you make the smoothest

6.8

transition possible (see FIGURE 6.9). Pretend the shaft is made out of very brittle glass, and that any sudden movement will shatter the glass.

- Focus on the top dimple (that is, the North Pole) of the ball as you swing through. This will keep your posture tall, promoting ball-first contact (see FIGURE 6.10).

- If you have 80 or 90 yards to the pin, take less loft than normal (say, an 8-iron vs. a pitching wedge) and swing longer back and through (in other words, from 10 to 2 o'clock) at the same slow pace.

6.9

6.10

What if... The ground under your ball is as hard as cement?

Off hardpan, the goal remains to make ball-first contact, although in this instance you will dig into the ground just slightly after impact. For this to happen, you'll need to have lively wrists for this shot and put them to work. Set up with the ball back in your stance and even more weight on your front leg. To ensure that your weight is left, look at the target side of the ball at address and lift your right heel about a quarter of an inch off the ground. Cock your right wrist going back, and keep it hinged for as long as you can on the downswing. This is key: Provided the right wrist remains slightly bent back and the handle is forward at impact, the clubhead will contact the ball and then the ground, trapping the ball against the turf (see FIGURE 6.11). The leading edge of the club should dig in somewhat, creating a small divot on the target side of the ball.

6.11

Ball up against Tree

As I discussed earlier in chapter 1, the clubface is much more influential than the path in determining where the ball goes. It's 70 to 80 percent responsible for the initial starting direction of the ball's flight. Knowing this bit of information is the secret to hitting this shot.

Seve has no chance to make his normal backswing here, because the tree is in the way. Nor can he swing directly at the target, which is the flagstick located just behind his right shoulder. But if he shuts the clubface (see FIGURE 6.12) and positions his body on an angle 45 degrees to his target, he can not only make a backswing, but he can start the ball in the general direction of his target. Seve swings the club on a path (his shoulder plane) that's 45 degrees to the right of his target (see FIGURE 6.13), but since he has the clubface

6.12

6.13

pointing just a few feet right of the flagstick, the ball will come out relatively straight, in the direction of the flag. Again, the clubface has more influence over the shot's starting direction than the path does.

The downside to shutting the face is that the ball isn't going to come out with much backspin; hence, you're going to have to allow for some roll, and perhaps play the shot short of the green. In this particular instance, Seve had a lot of green to the right of the flagstick to work with, which made the shot much more manageable.

What if ... The ball is several feet from the tree, allowing for some type of backswing—albeit not a full one?

In any restricted swing situation where there's a tree, some branches, or a fence impeding your swing, you have to make sure there's enough room to attempt some kind of backswing. You can't make the club go straight up and down like an elevator, although with a few setup adjustments you can reduce the width of your swing somewhat. Take a few slow-motion practice swings to the side of the ball to see what kind of space there is.

Once you determine there's enough room to make a backswing, position your body so that the ball is way back in your stance, behind your right foot. You want your head and most of your upper body in front of the ball (see FIGURE 6.14). Grip down on the handle, and take a few more slow-motion practice swings to gauge how much you must cock your wrists on the backswing to avoid the tree. Pick up the club very abruptly on the backswing, cocking your wrists to the degree you rehearsed on your practice swings. Your arms shouldn't swing much at all on the backswing; it's just a sharp, upward cocking of the wrists (see FIGURE 6.15).

Chop down on the back of the ball, swinging in the direction of your target. The ball will come out low and run hard, so make sure the ground between you and the target is relatively firm, not covered with thick, lush grass.

6.14

6.15

MARTIN'S KEYS

- Choose a stance that will allow you to make a backswing, and set your knees, hips, and shoulders parallel to this stance line.

- Close the clubface abruptly to your stance line, so that it points more or less in the direction of your target (that is, where you want the ball to finish).

- Swing along your body/stance line, allowing the club to work on a flattish plane on both the backswing and the follow-through. Do not try to steer or manipulate the face in any way; trust your setup adjustments and make your normal swing for a shot of that distance, remembering that the ball will come out low and roll quite a bit on the ground.

Low-Flying 6-Iron Punch Shot

Unless you're adept at hitting a lot of fairways, this is a shot you're bound to face from time to time. The distance may vary (Seve looks to have about 100 yards to the flagstick in this photo), but the goal remains the same: hit the ball high enough to get out of trouble, but low enough so that you don't clip any overhanging tree branches. The last thing you want is to have the ball shoot back at you, sending you even deeper into the trees.

The mistake most amateurs make when trying to keep the ball low is that they take too little loft. They pull out their 3- or 4-iron and punch the ball out from the trees, only there's not enough loft on the club to get the ball back to the fairway—or onto the green. The ball gets caught up in the rough and goes virtually nowhere. Another common mistake you'll see with recreational golfers is that they'll use a lofted club, put the ball back in their stance, and swing normally. Oftentimes, they'll make better contact than they do from the fairway, but will launch the ball too high into the branches above.

To make the cleanest escape possible, you want to use your 6- or 7-iron and take loft off it by adjusting both your setup (weight left, hands well forward) and your swing (three-quarter backswing with an abbreviated finish). With Seve, note how his hands are still well ahead of the clubhead after impact, and that he's taking a fairly big divot (see FIGURE 6.16). This

6.16

means there's a lot of shaft lean on the ball at impact, and the clubhead is swinging down into the ground on a fairly sharp angle—which delofts the face even more. Another thing to note is how open his stance is to the target line. Whenever you play the ball well back in your stance with a steep downward below, the path of the swing will be to the right of your foot line when you make contact, and there's a good chance the clubface will also be looking to the right. This is because the clubface makes contact with the ball before it has a chance to return to square (on its arc); therefore, you just open your stance to start the ball on line. The window to get the ball out is fairly small, so the last thing you want to do is hit this shot anything but straight.

MARTIN'S KEYS

- Play the ball back in your stance, opposite your right foot, with your weight strongly favoring your front side. You want to have the feeling that you're delofting the clubface at address, which you get by moving your hands well ahead of the ball (see FIGURE 6.17). The grip end of the club should point at your left hip or just outside the hip.

- Swing your arms back to 9 or 10 o'clock with a fair amount of wrist hinge, so that your arms and club shaft form a letter "L." Have the clubface looking at the ball for a good portion of the backswing and then at the target for much of the

6.17

What if... There's no going around the tree, and the only way is up (over the tree)?

You should try this shot only as a last resort, when all other routes have been blocked. It's extremely high risk because it requires a lot of clubhead speed, and should you fail, there's no telling where the ball may wind up. Some say you can hit it through the tree, because trees are 90 percent air, but so is a screen door. So don't be surprised when that 10 percent jumps up and bites you. Make sure you have a decent lie, because if you can't slide the club underneath the ball, it's going to be difficult to hit it high. Also, look at the depth of the tree or cluster of trees you're trying to carry. If it's thick up there, you may want more club than you initially think (for example, a 9-iron vs. a pitching wedge), so that the ball has enough forward momentum to scale the tree (or trees).

6.18

To get the height you need, play the ball more forward in your stance than normal, so that your hands are ever so slightly behind the ball. Your weight should favor your right side (about 60–40), with your feet and shoulders pointing left of the target line. (The higher the shot, the more you want to open your stance and put cutspin on the ball.) Imagine you're tossing a ball underhanded over an imaginary hedge that's about 15 feet high. Make as big and wristy a swing as you can, throwing the clubhead under the ball with a tremendous amount of speed. Finish high, with your hands at or above your left shoulder (see FIGURE 6.18). The higher the finish, the better job you did using your wrists and accelerating the club through impact.

follow-through. This is one swing in golf where you don't want much face rotation going back or coming through.

- Swing down and through the ball, with your hands leading the clubhead into impact. Abbreviate your finish, stopping when your left arm is at about 4 o'clock on the follow-through. At this point, the clubhead should still be lower than your hands, which can happen only if the hands beat the club to the ball. You want to have the feeling that the clubhead never passes the hands on this shot.

Intentional Hook around a Tree

On a day when there was an albatross (often referred to as a double eagle) and two hole-in-ones, the lasting image from the final round of the 2012 Masters was that of Bubba Watson carving a miraculous hook shot from out of the woods on the second playoff hole. Watson, 150 yards from the flagstick and a good 20 yards into the trees, managed to curve the ball some 40 yards and carry a bunker, landing the ball within 10 feet of the hole. And he did it with a gap wedge! The ensuing two-putt par was good enough for his first major title.

The amount of hook that Seve puts on the ball in the sequence of photos here (see FIGURES 6.19, 6.20, and 6.21) isn't 40 yards, but it's not far off, judging by where he's looking in the final photo. To hit a hook of this magnitude, you must first draw a fairly clean lie. If the ball is sitting down in the rough, you're not going to get enough club on the ball to make it curve. You also need to get the toe of the club to the ball first to impart the necessary hookspin on it. In the final image, it's apparent Seve has done this—his right hand has rolled over the left, his right palm pointing somewhat at the ground (see FIGURE 6.21). The face of the club is pointing left of the big tree as well. Judging by where his body is aimed (right of the tree)

6.19

6.20

6.21

and where the clubface is pointing at the completion of his swing, it appears as if Seve has hit a sweeping hook around the big tree to the fairway that runs nearly parallel to his stance line.

MARTIN'S KEYS

- Aim your body (feet, hips, shoulders) well right of the tree you're trying to hook the ball around, and aim the clubface at a point halfway between the tree and your stance line.

- Swing along your stance line, well to the right of the tree, but have the feeling that the toe of the club is speeding up and overtaking the heel through impact. Try to make your forearms touch on the follow-through, which encourages the right forearm to roll over the left through impact.

- As an image, picture a tree about a foot in front of your ball, and stick the toe of the clubhead into its trunk as you swing through (see FIGURE 6.22). This will help you rotate the clubface into a closed, or hook, position.

What if... The ball settles under a bush about 15 yards from the green?

Most golfers would settle for just punching the ball out from under a bush, but you do have another option: You can hit the shot from your knees. This allows you to swing the club on a fairly flat plane, so you can take a bigger swing and hit the ball with enough force to perhaps knock it on the green.

If you attempt this shot, don't make the mistake of going down to the ground with a 6- or 7-iron. With the toe so far off the ground, you won't be able to get enough of the clubface on the ball to hit it hard enough. Instead, opt for a club with a much flatter lie angle, less loft and more meat behind the face, such as your 3-wood or driver. Swing the club back almost parallel to the ground, on the same flat angle as the club shaft (see FIGURE 6.23). As you swing through, feel as if you're hitting down on the ball, as in a chip or a pitch shot (see FIGURE 6.24). This is key: If the clubhead comes in too level, it's likely to find the ground behind the ball. Hit down on the ball with the clubhead, and it should pop through the other side and roll toward the green like a chip.

6.23

6.24

Short-Game Skills and Practice Drills

Some of my fondest memories as a child involved sneaking onto the 7th green at Newcastle Golf Club each evening and playing a game of "My Castle" with my good friend Mike Hassall. The contest was similar to the popular basketball-shooting contest called "Around the World." We'd hit all types of crazy short-game shots, and whoever got the ball up-and-down in the fewest number of strokes got to choose what the next shot would be.

Sometimes we'd try to knock the ball off a nearby tree, seeing who could land it on the green closest to the hole. Other times, because Mike was a left-hander, we'd switch clubs and play the shot from the other's perspective. Because my house backed up to the course, we'd simply hop the fence and start playing our games the minute the last group passed through. We'd chip and putt for hours, until it was pitch-black and we couldn't see the ball 2 feet in front of us.

I'm sure if you polled some of the best short-game players in the world today, they'd have a similar story to tell. Tiger Woods is a good example. As a young toddler growing up in California, he learned the game on the putting and chipping green. As he got older, he started to work back toward the tee, spending more time on his full swing, but he never got tired of practicing the short game. The kid in him still enjoys that part of practice the most.

"I don't like hitting balls," said Woods. "I'd much rather chip and putt all day. Putting is fun. Chipping is fun. Hitting balls and working on stuff, it's like eating your vegetables. You've got to do it, but you don't have to like it."

Most recreational golfers have a different attitude toward short-game practice. They'd rather stand on the range for hours, devouring one pyramid of balls after another. They find short-game practice to be boring, nothing like the fun Tiger described it as. But that's only because they make it boring. To get the most out of your short-game practice, you have to make it challenging. You need to simulate the types of situations you'll encounter on the course. When Raymond Floyd was a kid, he used to search for the most impossible lie he could find around the green and then try to find a way to get the ball up and down from that lie. Luke Donald's earliest memory as a kid was "throwing 10 balls around the green in the most difficult lies, and trying to get them up and down, pretending to be Seve."

If you still find that the fun is missing from your short-game practice, then make it competitive. Play games with your friends or fellow competitors, as Seve used to around the chipping green and the clubhouse with the other Spanish players on Tour. It might seem like fun to pound your driver on the range for hours, but that is not going to make you a better player. If you want to improve, and improve quickly, then you have to spend at least 50 percent of your practice time on your short game. A decent long game only determines how high your score is going to be, whereas the short game determines how low it's going to be.

Here are nine practice drills/games you can play on your own or with a friend, along with six skills/hand-eye coordination drills. These games and drills will not only improve your feel and touch around the greens, but they'll help you develop the hand-eye coordination skills necessary to make solid contact on a consistent basis. Not only will your short game and putting skills improve dramatically, but you'll have some fun in the process. Who knows, you might start liking short-game practice as much as Tiger does.

Putting Games

The following three drills were devised by Dr. Rick Jensen, an internationally recognized performance consultant and sports psychologist based in the West Palm Beach area.

Speed Control

Find a flat, straight putt with no break to it, and place a tee down at a distance of 6 feet from the hole. Hit nine putts from that spot, alternating speeds so that the first ball banks off the back of the cup (see FIGURE 7.1), the second one drops in the middle of the cup, and the third one falls just over the front edge of the cup. Some people would refer to this as "dying" the ball into the cup. Log the number of putts you make at the correct speed. The Tour standard is 9 out of 9. The purpose of this drill is to show you what the best speed is for you to hole the most putts.

7.1

Four Corners

Find an area of the practice green with some slope to it, and place four tees around the hole at a distance of 3 feet. One tee should represent an uphill putt, and the others right-to-left, downhill, and left-to-right. Place one ball down at each tee. Start at the uphill tee, and try to make the putt from that tee. Once you've done that, move counterclockwise to the next 3-foot tee, and repeat. Should you miss, you have to start all over from the uphill tee. Repeat until you've gone around the whole circle, making four consecutive putts (see FIGURE 7.2). Next, move each tee back 1 foot from its previous spot (to 4 feet), and again try to make four consecutive putts. Repeat again at 5 feet. If you really want to test yourself, see if you can make your way around the circle at 3, 4, and 5 feet, sinking

7.2

twelve consecutive putts. The purpose of this drill is to boost your confidence in your short-putting game and also make you a more athletic putter (in other words, you're not thinking about every stroke, you just do it.)

7.3

6-Foot Putting Ladder

Place seven balls in a straight line extending out from the cup, with the first ball at 6 feet and the others in 6-foot increments at 12, 18, 24, 30, 36, and 42 feet. Lay a club at a right angle to the target line, 3 feet behind the cup. Hit each putt, with the goal being to make it or have it finish between the hole and the shaft lying on the ground (see FIGURE 7.3). If any ball finishes short of the hole or rolls past the shaft, you have to pick up each ball you've putted up to that point and start all over again from 6 feet. See how far you can go back before missing. The Tour standard is 42 feet. Yes, they make it all the way back.

This is the ultimate lag putting drill. If you can consistently hit a 36-foot putt within the dimensions set forth in this drill, under the pressure of knowing you have to start over if you miss, you can do it on the course with relative ease. The perfect "make" speed for any mid- to long-range putt is one that finishes 18 inches past the hole (should it miss). This leaves you with an easy tap-in for your next putt. Work on this Ladder Drill each time you practice your putting, and you should find yourself three-putting a lot less.

Chipping and Pitching Games

Throwaway Drill

Find a spot about 5 yards off the green, and chip five balls to the same flagstick, trying to get each to finish within 3 feet of the hole (see FIGURE 7.4). If all five finish within this target

7.4

range, then throw one ball away and move on to a new location. Repeat, throwing one ball away as soon as you chip four consecutive balls within 3 feet of the pin. If any of the balls finishes outside the circle, then you have to start all over again from the beginning until you're able to chip each consecutively to within 3 feet. Continue under the same format, until you have only one ball left and you chip it close.

If you find this too difficult in the beginning, start at three balls. This drill, devised by Dr. Morris Pickens of the Sea Island Golf Learning Center, will certainly improve your chipping and distance control. Experiment with different clubs to see what combination of carry and roll makes it easiest to fit each ball within the tightest range of the hole.

Par 18

Using only one ball and whichever clubs you choose, play nine different holes around the green, until you've holed out on each (see FIGURES 7.5 and 7.6). Make the shots whatever you want. I normally start students with short chips before advancing to more difficult chips, pitches, and bunker shots. The better you get at the drill, the more difficult you make the shots. Each hole should be scored as a par 2. The goal is to play the course in even par (18) or less strokes, although you may find it difficult to achieve this at first. This drill, developed by Dr. Karl Morris, one of Europe's leading sports psychologists, really gets you to focus on the

7.5

7.6

shot at hand because there's a score attached to each shot. It simulates the scoring pressures that you face on the course. Perform this drill a number of times, and you should start to see yourself getting the ball up-and-down more often.

Two Ball, Worst Ball

Chip two balls to the same target (see FIGURE 7.7), and identify the worst of the two shots. Putt both balls out from this location (see FIGURE 7.8), and count the worst of the two strokes. In other words, if one putt should go in and the other one lip out, you have to score it as a 3, or bogey. Play eight additional holes, or shots, under the same scoring system, playing two balls from the worst of the initial two shots. You can attempt any short-game shot you like, from a chip to a high lob to a 40-foot putt. Each hole is scored as a par 2, so if you hole out, you record a birdie, and if it requires three shots, you card a bogey. Tally up your score at the end of 9 holes to see if you can come even close to par. This exercise helps you identify your bad shots, or

7.7

7.8

weak links, in the short game, so that you can focus more of your practice time on these areas and become a more consistent all-around performer in the future.

Hula Hoop Landing Spot Drill

Pick out a flagstick and a flat area of the green you want to land the ball on—usually, one to two paces onto the green. Lay a hula hoop (or I have my students use a product called the Golf Ring, as do a lot of Tour pros; visit golfring.com) flat on the ground over this spot, and chip several balls into the circle (see FIGURE 7.9), trying to find the right combination of carry and roll (see FIGURE 7.10) that will consistently put you

7.9

7.10

close to the hole. Sometimes you'll have to try several different clubs before you find something that works; other times you'll have the right club, but will have chosen the wrong landing spot. Remember: the flatter the landing area, the more predictable the roll, and the more slope there is to the landing area, the less predictable that first bounce is going to be. Keep moving the hoop around and chipping to different hole locations. This exercise teaches you how to pick the right landing spot and also hit the right shot for the ball to finish near the hole. The best chippers are the ones who are aware of where to land the ball to produce the correct amount of roll.

Basket/Umbrella Drill

Place a large range bucket or basket down at 10 yards, and see if you can pitch a ball into the basket (see FIGURE 7.11). An upside-down umbrella, pictured, works just as well. Once you accomplish this, pace off 10 more yards and place the basket down at 20 yards, and repeat. Continue on to 30 and 40 yards, and stop whenever you find it too difficult to land the ball in the basket. This exercise heightens your awareness of distance and also of how much swing you need to make to produce a shot of 20 yards, 30 yards, and so on. It also teaches you how to make solid contact with your wedges, which is the only way to hit the ball high and soft enough—and with the right distance—to make it land in the basket.

7.11

Hula Hoop Drill #2

Join two shafts together and stick them in the ground, taping a hula hoop to the end so it forms an airborne circle that you can hit the ball through. You'll need to secure it with a lot of duct tape. Pace off 10 yards so that you're facing the hoop, and see if you can pitch the ball through the circle (see FIGURE 7.12).

7.12

Move back another 10 yards and repeat, and so on. Picture the shot in your mind's eye and the type of trajectory and landing angle you'll need to split the hula hoop. What type of adjustments will you have to make to your ball position, alignment, clubface, and technique to make the ball do what you want it to? Seve was one of the best ever at knowing what to do with the club and his body to make the ball match the trajectory he saw in his mind's eye.

Hand-Eye Coordination Drills

The following drills are designed to help you improve your hand-eye coordination, so that you can make solid contact more often. For golfers who struggle to hit the middle of the clubface, these drills will get you closer to doing just that on a consistent basis. Solid contact is one of my 7 Maxims for the Short Game (see chapter 1). The more consistent your contact is, the more reliable your distances will be.

Knock Its Legs Off

Tee a ball about an inch and a half off the ground (see FIGURE 7.13) and, using your sand wedge, see if you can knock the tee straight out from under the ball without touching the ball (see FIGURE 7.14). The ball should drop straight to the ground (see FIGURE 7.15). The more efficient you become at knocking the legs out from under the ball, the lower you push the tee into the ground until just the head of the tee is protruding above the earth. This drill teaches you how to slide the club under the ball, maintaining the true loft on the clubface so that the ball flies on a nice, high trajectory. It's perfect for hitting lob shots or any shot where you need to stop the ball with height.

7.13

7.14

7.15

159

7.16

Remove the Paint Line

Buy yourself a can of white spray paint, and lay down a line about two feet long, perpendicular to your stance line (that is, where the ball would be in your stance). Take a few practice swings with a wedge, seeing if you can knock the paint off the line. The deepest part of your divot might be on the target side of the line. Once you become proficient at hitting the line, then push a tee into the ground on the same line and practice hitting the tee, before finally advancing to a ball (see FIGURE 7.16). The purpose of this drill is to teach you how to bottom the club out in the correct place—at the ball or just forward of the ball. If the low point of your swing is consistently at the ball or slightly on the target side of the ball, then you're going to make solid contact and have very good distance control.

6-Iron Lob Shot

Seve learned how to hit a high lob using, of all things, a 3-iron. He figured out a way to pop the ball almost straight up in the air and land it softly, even with about a third of the loft of a sand wedge. I'm not going to ask you to use a 3-iron, because most golfers today don't carry one, but take out your 6-iron and see if you can figure out, as Seve did, how to slide the clubhead under the ball and loft it gently into the air.

7.17

If you need some help, make the following adjustments. First, make sure the ball is forward of center in your stance, similar to where you'd play a mid-iron or a hybrid. Lay the handle of the club back so that the shaft points at your right hip, and your hands are well behind the ball (see FIGURE 7.17). Widen your stance, so that your hands are even lower to the ground, and lay the clubface back as flat as possible. Point your body left of the target, and swing along your shoulder line. Feel as if you're cutting the legs out from underneath the ball. All of these setup adjustments should help you slide the club under the ball and turn that 6-iron of yours effectively into a high-lofted club (see FIGURE 7.18).

7.18

This a great exercise because it helps you understand what you have to do to the club, your setup, and your body to create an extra-high, soft shot. If you can make a 6-iron fly high in the air and stop fairly quickly, imagine what you can do with a 60-degree wedge!

Thumbs and Forefingers

Grip the club with just the thumbs and forefingers of each hand (see FIGURE 7.19), and swing it back and through with only these four digits on the club. This advanced version of the lob shot makes it super-easy to slide the clubhead under

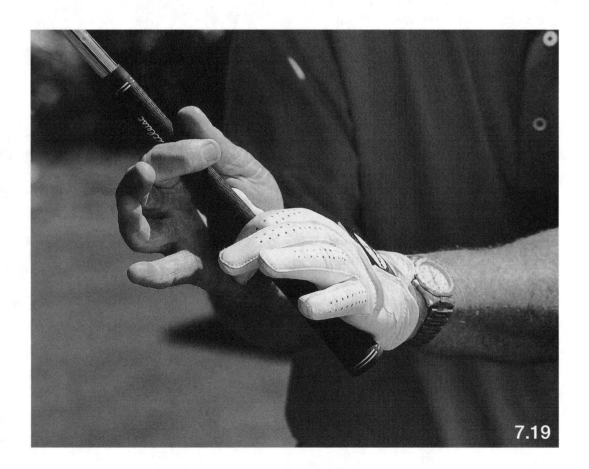

7.19

7.20

the ball (see FIGURE 7.20), adding more loft to the shot. You'll have no other option but to keep your grip pressure light and loose, which prevents any re-gripping or additional tension during the swing. You should get a feel for how the clubhead passes the hands early and the clubface points upward at the sky after impact.

Tap Two Shafts

Hold one club in each hand by the head of each club. Make sure both clubs are similar in length, such as a 6- and a 7-iron, or a 9-iron and a pitching wedge. Swing the grip end of each club away from you (see FIGURE 7.21) and then try to tap them together, almost as if you were clapping hands (see FIGURE 7.22). Continue in this windshield wiper–like motion, tapping the

7.21

7.22

shafts together near your feet. You'll find that it's not very easy at first, and that it takes very good hand-eye coordination to get them to touch on a consistent basis.

One Leg, One Hand

Stand on just your left leg, holding the club in the opposite (right) hand. Put your left arm behind your back, and set up to a ball as if you were going to hit a 20-yard chip shot. Make your normal chip swing with your right arm only, making a smooth transition into the forward swing. If you try to add any extra or unnecessary acceleration to the club with your right arm through impact, or if there's any jabbing or flipping at the ball, you're likely to lose your balance and flub the shot. But if you allow gravity to take over and let the clubhead drop onto the back of the ball, you should make solid contact (see FIGURE 7.23). You also need to have very good hand-eye coordination, because your balance is less than ideal. Repeat the drill, only this time switch things around so that you're standing on your right leg and swinging with only your left arm.

7.23

Afterword

recently had the opportunity to ask Tiger Woods, arguably one of the best short-game players of this era, what made Seve Ballesteros so special. And he recalled a conversation he had with Seve that lasted several hours—about one club (a 56-degree sand wedge)!

"It was pretty cool how he'd get the ball to spin sideways, or how he'd get that extra roll, why he'd do it," explained Woods. "And then he'd go out and do it. He was the best. He understood what the clubhead did through the ground better than anybody else. Not just how to deliver it correctly, but what his body needed to do and how the club was going to react, and what kind of spin it was going to produce."

My hope in writing this book is first to honor my hero, the brilliant Seve Ballesteros, and to also help you with your short game because, as Tiger said, nobody did it better than Seve. He had the ability to land the golf ball like "a butterfly with ballet shoes," with a skill and an imagination matched by no one. Through the photos and information in this book, you now have the knowledge to hit a wide array of short-game shots, from the routine (basic running chip) to the unordinary (bayonet shot from a plugged lie in the bunker), with insights on how Seve played many of them.

While this book doesn't cover every eventuality and situation in the short game, it does touch on most. There's a ton of useful information in here that I spent a lifetime compiling, observing the likes of Seve, Tiger, Gary Player, and many of the game's greatest short-game players. The instruction in this book will make you better, and it will help you save two or three shots (or more) per round—that is, if you don't try to apply it all at once. If you read *Houdini Shots* in one sitting and then try to put all fifty-plus shots into play immediately, you're going to create one giant headache for yourself.

One of my teaching mantras is that you cannot fix what you do not understand. I hope you now understand the technique involved in hitting a wide variety of short-game shots. Digest each skill one by one and take the time to practice and learn each one of them as you expand your arsenal of shots.

Finally, I would like to end *Houdini Shots* with the following eight-point recap and wish you the best in creating some of your own magic on the golf course.

1. To get better, you have to work hard on the right things. Simply putting in the effort isn't going to move the needle; you have to allocate your time diligently, practicing

the things—such as the hand-eye coordination drills in chapter 7—that will allow you to improve faster.

2. The single most important skill you need to develop to become a great short-game player is to learn how to make consistently solid contact.

3. Choose a club wisely, being mindful that the easiest way to control a shot's distance is to keep the ball along the ground. Don't always reach for one club (i.e., your sand wedge), as poor players so often do.

4. When chipping, pitching, or hitting bunker shots, always pick out a spot where you want to land the ball.

5. Always swing the club on a plane that matches your shoulder line, realizing that this plane isn't always directed at the target.

6. Remember that the ball will start its flight—or roll, if it's a putt—in the general direction where the clubface is pointing at impact.

7. Use your imagination, and consider every option that's available to you. On one occasion Seve hit the most remarkable of bunker shots from a severe downslope under the back lip of a greenside bunker. This prompted his playing partner to ask, "Whenever did you practice that?" To which Seve replied, "Never, I just thought it might work." That's using your imagination.

8. The lie of the ball dictates what's possible. Even Seve couldn't do the impossible, but sometimes he got really close.

Good luck!
—Martin Hall

INDEX